LEARNING TO GRIEVE

Foreword

This book provides an important contribution in helping teachers and students learn about a part of life which has previously often been considered taboo.

With heightened awareness over recent decades of the importance of open discussion of death, dying, grief and loss, the matter has now increasingly appeared in educational curricula and has been a source of open discussion in schools. Nevertheless, there are many settings in which adolescents in particular, but also children and other young people, find it very difficult to both express their distress and have it recognised and supported.

The range of difficulties that can arise for a young person who is grieving is highlighted in this book and there is a constructive learning approach for teachers and students to tackle this in the curriculum, incorporating grief and loss as a normal part of human growth and development.

Importantly this book is a helpful, constructive and positive approach. It sets a clear framework for learning about loss and grief with an innovative creative approach.

The authors are to be strongly commended on the work they have put together in this important volume.

Professor Beverley Raphael
Head, Department of Psychiatry
The University of Queensland

Geoffrey T. Glassock
Louise Rowling

LEARNING TO GRIEVE

Life Skills for Coping with Losses

For High School Classes

MILLENNIUM BOOKS

> **Notice:** Purchase of this book carries with it permission to reproduce the **WORKSHEETS** for student use. (No other part of this text may be reproduced without prior written permission of the publisher.)

If you are interested in an In-Service Day on how to use this text most effectively, contact

> Dr Geoffrey Glassock
> P.O. Box 460
> Lane Cove, NSW 2066
> Fax: (02) 427 4668

These Workshops can be organized for clusters of schools in NSW, and other States depending on numbers interested.

First published in 1992 by
Millennium Books, an imprint of
E.J. Dwyer (Australia) Pty Ltd
3/32–72 Alice Street
Newtown NSW 2042
Australia

Copyright © 1992 Geoffrey T. Glassock & Louise Rowling

This book is copyright. Apart from any fair dealing for the purposes of private study, research, criticism or review, as permitted under the Copyright Act, no part may be reproduced by any process without written permission. Inquiries should be addressed to the publisher.

National Library of Australia
Cataloguing-in-Publication data

Glassock, Geoffrey T.
  Learning to grieve.

ISBN 0 85574 896 6.

1. Grief – Study and teaching (Secondary). 2. Thanatology.
3. Loss (Psychology) – Study and teaching (Secondary). 4.
Adjustment (Psychology) – Study and teaching (Secondary).
I. Rowling, Louise. II. Title.

Cover, text and illustrations by Trevor Hood.
Typeset in 12/14 pt Palatino by Post Typesetters, Qld.
Printed by Southwood Press, NSW.

Contents

▸ Section 1
Years 7-10

Introduction — 1
Aim — 1
Teachers — 2
Teaching/learning Context — 2
Evaluation — 3
Critical incidents and the school — 3

Unit 1: Loss and change

Lesson
1. Life events as loss experiences — 7
2. Coping with change — 11
3. Losses experienced in changing family relationships — 14
4. Coping with divorce/separation — 17

Unit 2: The impact of death

Lesson
5. Introduction to fear of death — 19
6. *Extension lesson* — dealing with fears and fantasies — 21
7. Understanding death — 22
8. Expressing sympathy — 24
9. Judging death — 26
10. Explaining loss to children — 28
11. *Extension lesson* — a study of a cemetery — 29
12. Past reactions to loss — 31
13. The media's coverage of death — 32
14. The creative impetus of death — 36
15. The disposal of pets — 37
16. Responding to death — 39
17. Funerals and burial practices — 41

Unit 3: Exploring your own death

Lesson
18. Past, present and future — 43
19. *Extension lesson* — the changes that can be expected in later life — 47
20. Living life now — 48
21. Own death awareness — 50
22. Being at your own funeral — 53

Unit 4: Grief support

Lesson 23. Qualities of a supportive friend — 54
24. Using people for support — 56
25. Being supportive — 59
26. Helping grieving adolescents — 61
27. Saying goodbye — 63

▶ Section 2
Years 11-12

Unit 5: Loss and grief

Lesson 28. Loss: a universal human experience — 67
29. Grief is normal — 71

Unit 6: The impact of death

Lesson 30. Understanding loss in response to death — 74
31. Accidental death — 76
32. Laughing at death — 83

Unit 7: Exploring your own death

Lesson 33. Death and dying — 85
34. The process of dying — 89
35. People living with and dying from AIDS (1) — 93
36. People living with and dying from AIDS (2) — 95
37. Developing an appreciation for life — 97
38. Death awareness — 99
39. Burials and cremations in Australia — 102

Unit 8: Grief support

Lesson 40. Helping grieving friends and relatives — 104

Unit 9: The big questions

Lesson 41. Self-destructive behaviour: suicide — 107
42. Euthanasia — 112
43. The quality of life — 115
44. Organ transplantation — 119

Resource list

Videos — 124
Books for Adolescents — 127
Books for Teachers and Parents — 128
Services — 129

Learning to grieve: Life skills for coping with losses

▶ Introduction

This book is based on the belief that grief is a normal part of life and that people can learn positive ways of coping with the loss which creates the grief. The book recognises that while the death of someone significant is the most painful and emotionally disturbing loss, other losses also can have a devastating impact on the person. Frequently this factor is overlooked.

As the title of this book suggests, the authors believe that learning to cope with loss and grief is a life skill, that there are ways in which we can help prepare young people for these inevitable experiences. The book then is an expression of the writers' own personal beliefs that preventative education is a necessity and that the educational system is the appropriate place to learn these life-enhancing skills.

We believe the quality of life of young people will be improved when they understand that experiencing loss is a normal part of life and that they can discover the means for coping. While this will not remove the pain associated with grief, it will provide strategies for dealing with their own hurt and more confidently and compassionately assisting others.

The need to include this course in the curriculum is the result of the changing society in which we live. In the past, young people were not sheltered from the experience of death. The inevitability of death was acknowledged and a response to it in terms of religious ritual was commonplace. This is not the case today. Young people have less first-hand experience with death and less skills for coping. Moreover the rapidly changing society of which they are a part means they are also subject to other kinds of losses.

▶ Aim

The aim of this book is to enable teachers who feel comfortable with the topics relating to loss and grief, death and dying to explore these issues with young people. The approach adopted in this book is derived from the research findings on the role of social support. The book further aims to teach young people the skills: to be supportive to others; to express feelings (and thereby gain emotional control); to perceive the need for and accept support. It is also the authors' belief that schools, as the main social institutions outside the family, need to provide supportive environments through personnel, policies and structures.

The lessons provide a framework which allows for schools which support a particular belief system or value orientation on these topics to include that in their lesson planning.

▸ Teachers

The following are some guidelines to be considered by those who may be interested in teaching in the area of loss and grief, death and dying:

1. The teacher must have come to terms with his/her own feelings about death and loss, and to have admitted not only their existence, but their full status in the dynamics of his/her total personality functioning.
2. The teacher needs to know about death and death education in order to teach it.
3. The teacher of death education needs to be able to use the language of death easily and naturally, especially in the presence of the young.
4. The teacher needs to be familiar with the sequence of developmental events throughout life, and to have a sympathetic understanding of common problems associated with them.
5. The teacher needs an acute awareness of the enormous social changes that are in progress and of their implications for changes in our patterns of death-related attitudes, practices, laws and institutions.

The teacher taking a course in loss and grief education should be aware of basic counselling techniques and crisis intervention strategies. Students will seek help once the topic of loss, and in particular death, is made a topic for open discussion. Teachers should familiarise themselves with additional support services available in the school, e.g., counsellor, school nurse, etc. and appropriate referral services in the community.

▸ Teaching/learning context

The nature of these lessons requires the existence or the development of an atmosphere in the classroom that involves:

- trust between students, and teacher and students;
- effective communication;
- a teacher skilled in creating participatory learning environments;
- openness, on the part of the students in terms of preparedness to share personal experiences; on the part of the teacher, to model this sharing in a sincere manner;
- sensitivity to individual developmental and emotional states.

The lessons that follow are prescriptive. It is the experience of the authors that where teachers are conducting lessons on sensitive issues, step-by-step lesson outlines can reduce anxiety and increase the teacher's preparedness to tackle various topics. The lessons are also flexible, thus teachers can either follow them assiduously or modify them, according to the needs of the students.

The majority of the lessons are language based — requiring verbal or written skills. The teacher skilled in the use of role-play, music or art should modify the lessons for those students whose language skills are not well developed.

Most of the lessons are based on a forty-minute period allocation. Teachers will judge for themselves, according to the pace at which the students work, whether material should be expanded or contracted, keeping in mind the need to bring the topic to a close at the end of each lesson.

Many of the lessons involve groupwork. It is expected that by the time a class reaches sensitive issues in their curriculum, they are proficient as group members. If not, the teacher should spend time developing the students' ability to work in groups.

While it is not anticipated that teachers will cover all the lessons, the sequence should be carefully considered. In most instances it would not be advisable to begin the topic by asking students to consider their own death.

▶ Evaluation

Each of the lessons has measurable objectives. Teachers will readily be able to evaluate whether students are able to demonstrate the acquisition of skills or knowledge. Less easy to assess is the affective domain. There are certain values, beliefs and attitudes that are implicit in the content and teaching/learning strategies presented in this book — for example, the belief that there is not a right or wrong way for people to grieve.

Additionally, it could be expected that encouraging students to share life experiences that have made an emotional impact on them will result in a classroom atmosphere of openness and trust, where supportive peer relationships are encouraged. Evaluating the extent of this achievement will involve some subjective judgement.

The following questions might aid the teacher:

- Are the students more able to share their experiences towards the end of the unit than at the beginning? What evidence have you of this?
- Have the students demonstrated their personal awareness of issues through verbal, written or visual means?
- Has the completion of unfinished sentences at the end of the lessons showed an increased perception and personal awareness by the students?
- Has there been an increased contact between the students and members of the pastoral care system in the school?
- Has there been any feedback from parents?

▶ Critical incidents and the school

The school population is frequently confronted by traumatic events when the whole school community is emotionally disturbed by what has occurred. The school can develop a process whereby these traumatic or critical incidents can be effectively managed.

Types of traumatic or critical incidents:
- the death of a parent, teacher or student;
- a serious accident, e.g. involving the school bus or during a school excursion;
- a natural disaster, e.g. floods, bush fires;
- sexual assault, rape, incest;
- school hold-up or arson involving school property;
- the suicide of a family member, teacher or student;
- the murder of a family member, teacher or student;
- the repossession of the family home, property or farm;
- a mass murder in the community.

Designing intervention strategies or disaster planning is necessary to assist the school community to deal with the situation. The management of the 'critical incident' will depend on the type and numbers of staff and/or students involved or affected. Many school administrators think that their school is immune from such things. The unfortunate reality is that no one is immune. Recent traumatic events in N.S.W. and other parts of Australia have clearly shown that 'life is unpredictable' and we are never quite sure when or where disaster will strike.

It would be useful therefore for the school to identify any situations which have the potential for creating a critical incident and then develop a plan of action for managing the incident. The following are some suggestions that a school could keep in mind in thinking about this task:

- Identify the person/s who will exercise control.
- Prepare the steps staff will take in response to the incident.
- If a debriefing is necessary, have a team of skilled people trained and available to lead groups in the process.
- Involve the school counsellor and/or school nurse.
- Identify the support services in the local community; ensure an up-to-date phone list is available.
- Delegate someone to deal with the media.
- Inform parents about the 'critical incident'.
- Provide literature to enable parents to deal with their children.

Depending on the nature of the incident and the degree to which the school is affected, it might be helpful to the school community to hold some kind of 'service' to enable staff and students to express their grief — especially when a death has occurred. Similarly with other kinds of disasters the school may need to find an appropriate way of corporately expressing its feelings etc.

▶ References

Management of Critical Incidents... A Guide for Schools, South Coast Region, Wollongong Department of Education, 1991.

Johnson, K., *Trauma in the Lives of Children*, Hunter House, California, 1989.

Traumatic Incidents Affecting Schools, Guidance and Counselling Services, Department of Education, Queensland, 1990.

▶ *Section 1*

YEARS 7-10

UNIT 1: LOSS AND CHANGE

Life events as loss experiences

▶ Objectives

At the end of this lesson the students will be able:
- to identify the changes experienced through life;
- to categorise their own losses in terms of the impact on their lives.

▶ Content

Introduce the topic by saying, 'Today we are going to talk about some life events that have occurred to all of us and look at how these have affected us.'

Ask the class to think about something that has happened in their lives that they think changed them. If necessary give some examples. The students are to write the event down, trying to describe how they felt and what impact they think this event had on their lives. Ask the class if anyone would like to share what they have written down. After 2 or 3 responses inform the class that sometimes change involves losses, e.g., moving house means that you may lose contact with friends or parental divorce may mean financial loss. Ask the class, 'What are some of the expected changes in our lives that have a negative impact, that is, are expected losses?' Record these on the board. Ask, 'What are some changes that are unexpected?' 'What can you lose as a result of these experiences?' Losses may involve a person, an object, a dream etc.

Present the class with the definition of loss experiences on an overhead projector or by writing it on the board.

> "A loss reaction occurs when anything that is valued or anyone we are attached to, is removed from our lives."

Thus a loss reaction can occur to many changes in our lives.

UNIT 1: LOSS AND CHANGE

On the board write the heading 'loss reaction' and ask the class to state any reaction they can remember having to the event they have written — it could be the feelings they wrote down that they had at the time. As the class responds, record their reactions under the physical, emotional and behavioural columns. (These headings could be put on the board or added later.) Possible responses could include:

Physical	Emotional	Behavioural
felt sick	sad	crying
headache	angry	got into fights
couldn't sleep	felt worthless	stopped eating

Say that these reactions differ between different people and different events that have occurred to them. What is important is that we acknowledge that something significant has happened and what we are experiencing is a normal reaction to the event.

The students are given Worksheet 1, which has a time line on it. They are to think back to losses they have had in their lives. Beginning with the earliest loss they can remember experiencing, the students are to mark the event on the time line and write a few sentences relating to what they can remember of the event. 'Describe anything that might have frightened you about this loss. What were the physical, emotional and behavioural responses?'

Divide the class into groups; then each person shares one life event with the group.

▸ Conclusion

The teacher reads the story *The Tenth Good Thing about Barney* (Judith Viorst. New York, Atheneum, 1971). If time is available ask the class why it helped to think of ten good things about Barney. Tell the class to think about the life events they experienced and for the next week try to identify what things helped them to cope.

▸ Extension Work

Recalling their list of loss experiences, tell the students that when thinking about the feelings we have, it is important to remember the following:

UNIT 1: LOSS AND CHANGE

1. that feelings are neither good nor bad
2. our feelings are unique
3. people can have different feelings at the same time.

Write the following on the board or overhead. Ask the students to think about one of the loss experiences they have listed and complete some or all of the following unfinished sentences:

1. If only I had ....
2. It was my fault that ....
3. I'm sorry that ....
4. I'm angry at ....
5. I've stopped blaming myself for ....
6. I'm glad that ....
7. I'm relieved that ....
8. The happiest memory I have of .... is ....

Divide the class into the same groups as earlier to share any of these sentences. The students should be permitted to pass if they do not feel able to share their feelings at this stage.

Worksheet 1

My Loss Experiences

My earliest loss was ....

Age

My most recent loss was ....

Complete this worksheet giving details of particular ages of your own loss experience. For example: Age 8, moved house and had to leave my best friend; still miss talking to him.

UNIT 1: LOSS AND CHANGE

YEARS 7-10

Coping with change

▶ Objectives

At the end of the lesson the students will be able:
- to identify both positive and negative outcomes of change;
- to describe a range of developmental losses.

▶ Content

Ask the class to recall the life events they listed on their time lines last lesson. Ask the class to think of the positive and negative changes that occurred because of these life events. On the board or overhead projector record these. Tell the class that one of the reasons the loss experiences we have can affect us so much is that they mean we are forced to alter things in our lives. Some people accept this and go about the sometimes very difficult task of changing, that is, they see change as positive, as part of our lifelong development. Other people find it too hard to change, that is, they view change negatively. This is why loss experiences are part of growing. They happen all through our lives.

Distribute another time line (Worksheet 2). The students are to think about life events involving loss that have occurred to older brothers and sisters, parents, grandparents, aunts, uncles... and to fill them in at a particular age, e.g., age 50 — grandmother's experience of death of husband, age 36 — uncle Tom lost his job.

Then take an event, such as separation and divorce, and ask students if this event is on their time line, what age they have recorded this against, if it has occurred in their families. (A wide range of ages can be expected.)

Ask the class to give the age at which they have recorded 'death of partner or spouse'. 'If you have recorded someone who was aged about 40, how did they react? If they were aged about 70, how did they react?' By asking the class what they notice about the ages recorded, it should become obvious that events happen at different times in people's lives and the people involved can react in similar and different ways. Some events that occur are predictable, e.g., moving from primary to high school, but some happen without warning. Tell the class that hearing about others' experiences may allow us to be better prepared for them should they occur in our lives.

Unit 1: Loss and Change

Ask the class to recall their homework and to think about ways they coped with the life event. (It could be expected at this stage that there may be minimal insight into strategies they used.) 'Were there some things that other people did that helped you?' (Further exploration of this will occur in Lesson 23.)

▶ Conclusion

Have the class complete the unfinished sentences and share whatever they wish with a partner.

My Family's Loss Experiences

Complete this worksheet giving brief details of particular ages of loss experiences of family members. For example, age 21, brother's girlfriend killed. Age 45, Aunt Mary's husband died; she did not go out of the house for two weeks.

▶ Sentence completions

1. The loss event I remember the most is ....
2. Changes that have happened in my family since then are ....
3. Changes that have happened in me are ....
4. Changes that have happened in Mum ....
5. Changes that have happened in Dad ....
6. Changes that have happened in my brothers ....
7. Changes that have happened in my sisters ....
8. Changes that have happened in my grandparents ....
9. Changes that have happened in my friends ....
10. Changes I don't like ....
11. Changes I do like ....
12. The memory I like best is ....

Worksheet 2

UNIT 1: LOSS AND CHANGE

Losses experienced in changing family relationships

▶ Objectives

At the end of this lesson the students will have:
- identified a range of feelings and losses experienced by family members at the time of parental separation;
- expressed a range of opinions about divorce.

▶ Content

Introduce the topic by asking the class 'How many of your families have experienced separation or divorce — parents or grandparents, aunts or uncles...'? For all people involved there are a range of feelings experienced and things 'lost', e.g., contact with friends or family. Brainstorm and record on the board feelings associated with divorce.

UNIT 1: LOSS AND CHANGE

Each student then writes a sentence describing one of the feelings, either what they — or a family member — experienced or what they imagine. Share these as a class or in small groups then relate these feelings to earlier lessons about grief.

Coping with separation and divorce, like death, takes time. Ask the class whether they think feelings change from the time of the initial information about the separation to a year or two later. 'Let's now think whether people are affected the same way or are there differences depending on age, gender and familial position, that is, parent, child, grandparent.

'Let's think of the people involved in separation and divorce. What losses do these people experience?' Record the brainstorm on the board.

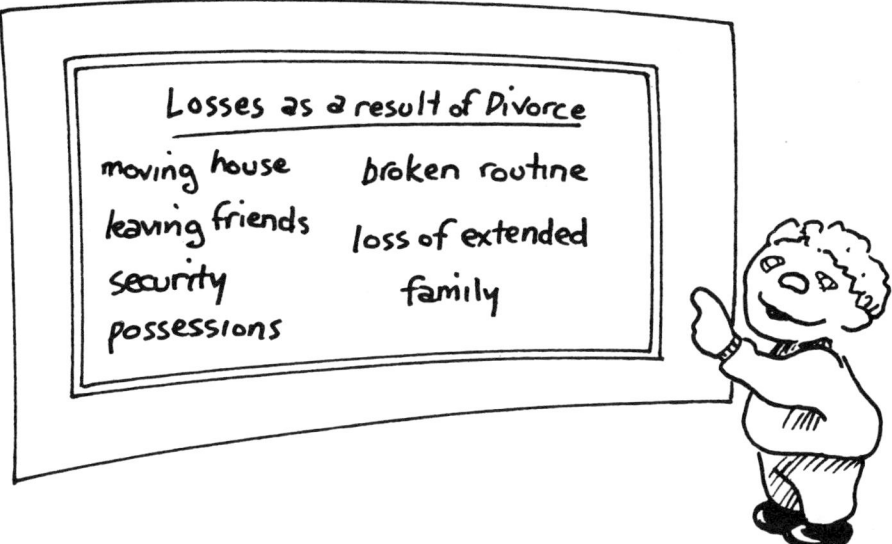

Distribute Worksheet 3. Ask the students to complete it individually, then divide them into groups to share. (Try to get an even spread of experiences and gender in each group.)

▶ Extension activity

Having discussed the issues in class, a panel of 'experts' can be selected to prepare answers for the next lesson — a mock television panel discussion. The chairperson can seek opinions from the panel then questions or comments can be called for from the class — television studio audience.

Worksheet 3

True/False Quiz	Agree	Don't Know	Disagree
Parents should stay together for the sake of the child.			
One parent is always to blame for the separation.			
It should be left to the Family Court to decide custody issues.			
Children of divorced parents should not be separated from each other.			
A single parent family is not as happy as a two parent family.			
It is easy for children to know when their parents are not getting on well together.			
It is easy to be a new family when a parent remarries.			

▸ Conclusion

Complete this sentence:

The most important thing I learnt from this lesson was

....

....

....

UNIT 1: LOSS AND CHANGE

Coping with divorce/separation

▶ Objectives

At the end of the lesson the students will have:

- listed some common problems experienced by adolescents whose parents are separated/divorced;
- identified some strategies to help adolescents cope with their parents' separation/divorce.

▶ Content

Ask the class to think of common problems experienced by adolescents whose parents are separated/divorced. For ideas, think about television shows that have handled this issue. Compile a list on the board.

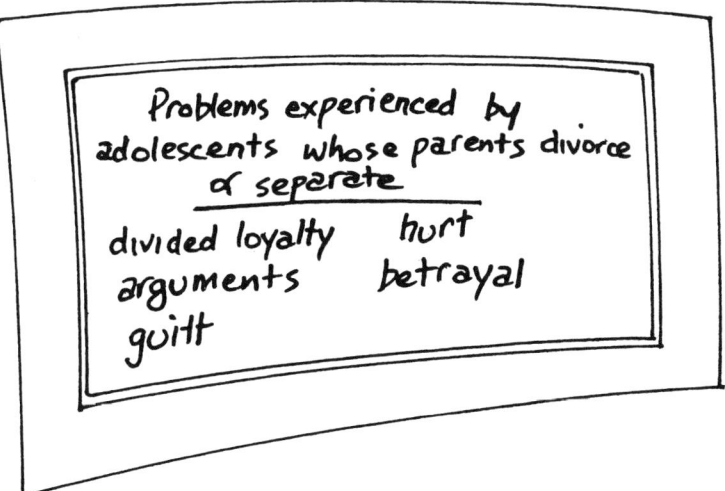

Divide the class into groups and allocate the problems equally. The groups discuss the problems and suggest ways adolescents can cope. Record solutions on large sheets of paper. Each group reports back to the whole class with responses being placed on the walls around the room.

Each group chooses a problem — a different one for each group — and expands upon it by writing a roleplay that includes roles for all the group members and shows at least one way in which the problem can be handled.

Unit 1: Loss and Change

▶ Conclusion

Groups are able to practise these roleplays and perform them for the rest of the class in the following lesson.

▶ Alternate Activity

Individual students select a problem and write a 'Dear Dolly' letter explaining the problem in detail. These are then 'posted' in a box and 'delivered' to someone in the class for reply. (The teacher may have written some letters prior to the lesson as examples and to give those students who work quickly, letters to which they might respond.)

▶ Conclusion

In pairs, one student reads out the letter and the other the reply. The class can discuss the particular solutions offered.

UNIT 2: THE IMPACT OF DEATH

YEARS 7-10

Introduction to fear of death

▶ Objectives

At the end of the lesson the students will be able:

- to identify how the use of language indicates a human being's fear of death;
- to identify euphemistic terms and phrases currently used to describe death;
- to discuss their fears and fantasies about death and develop strategies for dealing with these.

▶ Content

Tell the class, 'Today we are going to talk about a topic that is taboo in many families, that is, death'. The students then brainstorm words or phrases in common use that contain death and suggest the experience is bad, e.g., I could have died, I felt like death warmed up, he'll be the death of me.

Describe a euphemism as a substitution of an agreeable or inoffensive expression for one that may offend or suggest something unpleasant. Explain that different cultures may use different phrases to talk about death. The students then brainstorm words or phrases commonly used to describe death, e.g., passed on, called away, gone, sleeping, kicked the bucket, six feet under, on boot hill, turned their toes up, croaked.

Distribute Worksheet 4. Ask the class to complete questions 1-4. Discuss the responses as a class then have the students complete the unfinished sentences. Divide the class into groups and have them share any responses they wish to.

▶ Conclusion

Bring the class together and ask the students to share their responses giving reasons, where applicable, for their answers. Conclude by saying that while talking about death may be frightening to some, talking about fears and fantasies and bringing them out in the open helps make them less frightening.

Worksheet 4*

Circle the most appropriate response for you.

1. When you were a child how was death talked about in your family?
   a. openly
   b. with some discomfort
   c. only when necessary and then the children were excluded
   d. can't recall any discussion

2. In your opinion, at what age are people most afraid of death?
   a. up to 12 years
   b. 13 — 19 years
   c. 20 — 29 years
   d. 30 — 39 years
   e. 40 — 49 years
   f. 50 — 59 years
   g. 60 — 69 years
   h. 70 years and over

3. If people are afraid of death, do you think they are:
   a. afraid of the unknown
   b. fearful about how their own death will occur
   c. afraid of the pain they may experience with dying
   d. afraid of loneliness
   e. terrified of a 'state of not being'
   f. other ....

4. What does death mean to you?
   a. the end, the final process of life
   b. the beginning of life after death, a transition, a new beginning
   c. a joining of the spirit with some universal presence
   d. a kind of endless sleep
   e. termination of life, but with the survival of the spirit
   f. other ....

▶ Sentence completions

1. When I think of death I ....
2. My greatest fear about death is ....
3. When I die I would like to have at my bedside ....
4. When I die I will be proud that I ....
5. When I die I will be glad that when I was living I tried to ....
6. When I die I want people to say ....
7. Contemplating death has ....

* Adapted from E.S. Shneidman, 'Death Questionnaire', *Psychology Today*, Communications/Research/Machines, Inc., 1972.

UNIT 2: THE IMPACT OF DEATH

EXTENSION LESSON

Dealing with fears and fantasies

▶ Objective

At the end of this lesson the students will have:
- developed strategies for dealing with fears and fantasies.

▶ Content

Remind the class that last lesson they were talking about their fears relating to death. 'We all have fears, some relate to how we will die, or to being alone. I want you to think about a fearful dream you have had. I am going to read you a short excerpt about a teenage girl whose baby brother has died. She is having difficulty handling her grief.'

Read M. Pershall, *You Take the High Road*, p. 151.

Sometimes in dreams we are 'outside' it, that is, an observer. Sometimes we are a participant, that is, it is actually happening to us. 'Close your eyes, think yourself back into the fearful dream. Briefly describe in writing or by drawing, what is happening.'

After about 5 minutes, ask the class to close their eyes again and visualise a counterforce to overcome the person or thing that is feared. 'By doing this you will release some of the energy that you are using to repress the fear, that is, in being frightened. Describe in writing or drawing, your new stronger 'less fearful self, the person who has overcome the fear.'

UNIT 2: THE IMPACT OF DEATH

LESSON 7
YEARS 7–10

Understanding death

▶ Objectives

At the end of the lesson the students will:

- have presented graphically the age and gender of those who have died recently, using information from notices in the daily newspaper;
- have estimated a minimum number of grieving people in a community in a week by inference from notices in daily newspapers;
- be able to identify words and symbols associated with death.

▶ Content

Using the death and funeral notices in the daily paper for a week, in groups — one for each day — investigate the characteristics of those who have died.

1. Graph the spread of ages.
2. Graph males/females.
3. Identify a cause of illness, e.g., suddenly, after a long illness. (You assume they died of cancer if money is to be sent to the Cancer Foundation in lieu of flowers.)
4. Tabulate the number of relatives listed as the survivors. What can you conclude about the number of people who may be grieving in your town/city in the week you are studying the newspaper clippings?
5. Calculate the number of cremations and burials.

Present the major causes of death in Australia for different age groups (See Lesson 31). Compare the class's interpretation of the causes of death and ages with the statistics, e.g., were there indications that deaths for children and adolescents were due to accidents? Do the class's findings agree with the statistics?

Study the 'In Memoriam' section of the newspaper. Tabulate the number of notices according to the length of time since the death. Are there any patterns in this, e.g., longer/shorter time since the death of children who are being remembered in the notice? Who are the main people putting the notices in the newspaper — males, females, spouses, mothers, fathers etc. (You will need to look at the names — remembered by ...)

UNIT 2: THE IMPACT OF DEATH

▶ Conclusion

Write the following sentence on the board or overhead.
Get the students to complete it individually.
Then ask them to share their answers with the class.

From reading the 'Death', 'Funeral', and 'In Memoriam' notices in the newspaper I have learnt that...

UNIT 2: THE IMPACT OF DEATH

LESSON 8
YEARS 7-10

Expressing sympathy

▶ Objective

At the end of the lesson the students will be able:

- to devise a sympathy card using words and symbols of hope, peace and comfort.

▶ Content

Talk about various symbols of death, and list them on the board or overhead, e.g., coffin, mausoleum, skull, angels, cross, headstones, cemetery. Then give the class a few moments of silence to jot down the word or words that come to mind in connection with each symbol.

On a board, overhead projector or butcher's paper, compile a list of all the words. The class is asked to identify all those that relate to feelings. Ask the class if the words are mostly negative or mostly positive. 'What does that indicate about how we feel about death?'

'What are some symbols of hope, peace and/or love, e.g., a dove, flowers bursting into bloom, seeds germinating, sunrise.' Compile a list of words that suggest love, hope and peace.

Tell the class that in writing a letter or sympathy card you need to be honest. If you did not know the person well do not overdo the expression of sympathy, e.g., avoid 'deepest sympathy' or 'I share your anguish', saying rather 'I'm sorry to hear of the death of…'. Avoid phrases such as 'at least they did not suffer'; rather say 'your memories provide the thoughts of good times'. If appropriate make some personal reference, e.g., 'I remember when…'

UNIT 2: THE IMPACT OF DEATH

▸ Conclusion

Ask the students to design a sympathy card that utilises a positive symbol.

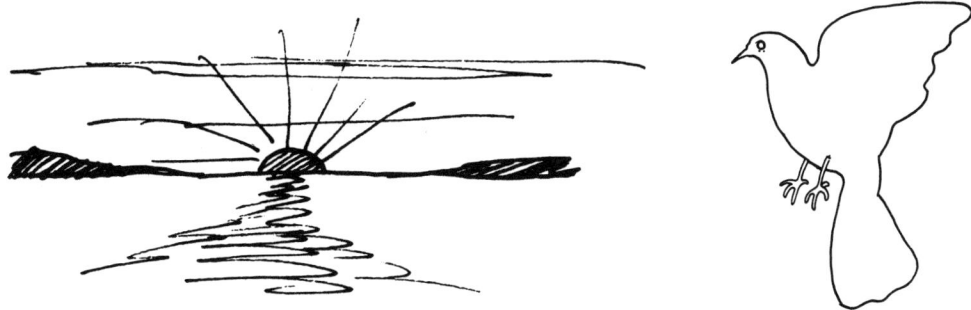

___Conclusion___

UNIT 2: THE IMPACT OF DEATH

LESSON 9
YEARS 7-10

Judging death

▶ Objective

At the end of the lesson the students will have:
- identified some of their beliefs about the appropriateness of death.

▶ Content

After a short introduction about death and dying (recapping on previous lessons) distribute Worksheet 5 to the students. It describes several ways people have died. The students are instructed to choose which, to them, would be the worst way to die. They will place the number 1 by the worst and so on, ending with number 8 — being the least unpleasant circumstances surrounding death. After the students have made their choices they form groups and share their rankings, giving reasons for their responses.

▶ Conclusion

Ask the class to identify some of the factors that influenced their decisions. These are recorded on the board under the heading 'the appropriateness of death'. Ask how they think it would influence their reaction if they had ranked an elderly person's death at number 8 and then their friend's grandparent dies. Remind the class that it is not the particular circumstances surrounding a death that are important, but the impact of the event on the bereaved. In other words, the death of an elderly person, even though he or she may have been ill for a long time, might have a special meaning for the bereaved. Conversely someone might be relieved when a relative dies, especially if the relative has been in a great deal of pain.

We need to encourage the bereaved to tell us about the death and in that way identify its impact on them.

Ranking Ways of Dying, from 1 (worst) to 8 (least unpleasant)

_____ 1. Susan. Aged 42.
She was shot by an intruder in her house.

_____ 2. Jim. Aged 88.
He was at home and died in his sleep after 13 years confined to his bed.

_____ 3. Ken. Aged 55.
He died suddenly of a heart attack right after he jogged 10 kilometres.

_____ 4. Marie. Aged 21.
She died after an unsuccessful kidney transplant. She had been on a dialysis machine for 5 years.

_____ 5. Doris. Aged 73.
She died in a nursing home exactly one year after her husband died.

_____ 6. Ralph. Aged 34.
He died when a drunk driver hit his car head-on. He leaves a wife and two young children.

_____ 7. Jane. Aged 16.
She died of an apparent suicide after a broken love affair.

_____ 8. Scott. Aged 17.
He died in a car crash after a celebratory party following his final high school exams.

Factors that influenced my choices:

_____

_____

_____

_____

Worksheet 5

UNIT 2: THE IMPACT OF DEATH

LESSON 10
YEARS 9-12

Explaining loss to children

▶ Objectives

At the end of the lesson the students will have:
- identified the necessary elements in a children's story that deals with loss;
- begun to write and illustrate a children's story that helps them understand the facts and feelings associated with loss experiences.

▶ Content

Bring two or three storybooks to class aimed at primary school age children. The books should contain stories that deal with children's loss experiences. Tell the class that it is about the age of eight that children have the capacity to understand what death is, although they do experience an emotional response to loss experiences at a much younger age. To have a mature concept of death children need to understand that death is inevitable, that is, it happens to everyone, and it is irreversible — you don't come back. Ask the class to identify some elements that could go in a story that explains loss to children, e.g., identifying areas covered in stories read to the class or the need to include references to physical, emotional and behavioural responses to loss. (See Lesson 1.)

Instruct the class that they are to write a children's story that describes a loss experience. Remind the students not to use euphemistic language and to be sure to describe the emotional responses of some of the characters in the story. They should decide on the age group at which they wish their story to be aimed and make the story no more than 10 pages of big printing, with about a paragraph per page. Depending on their skills the students may want to work in pairs, one writing and the other doing the illustrations.

▶ Conclusion

These books can be completed for homework and read to the whole class the following week. With the permission of the Principal, stories could also be shared with the local primary school.

UNIT 2: THE IMPACT OF DEATH

**LESSON 11
YEARS 7–10**

EXTENSION LESSON

A study of a cemetery

▶ Objectives

At the end of the lesson students will be able:

- to describe their thoughts and feelings as a result of walking around a cemetery;
- to state the role of cemeteries in recording family histories.

▶ Content

Visit a cemetery that is at least 100 years old. Ask the students to walk around for about 10 minutes, reading the tombstone inscriptions, not talking to anyone. Have them complete Worksheet 6.

▶ Conclusion

Encourage students to share their experiences.

Worksheet 6

1. Write down the thoughts and feelings you had as you walked around the cemetery.

   Thoughts ....
   ....
   ....

   Feelings ....
   ....
   ....

2. What does the cemetery tell you about the type of death of some of those buried there? Quote specific examples.

   ....
   ....
   ....

3. Can you work out any family history from the family plots, e.g. women who died in childbirth or infectious diseases that killed more than one child in a family. Give examples.

   ....
   ....
   ....

4. Is there a difference between old and new parts of the cemetery? If so, what is it?

   ....
   ....
   ....

5. Record the epitaph you like the most or draw the graveyard monument that appeals to you most.

   ....
   ....
   ....

UNIT 2: THE IMPACT OF DEATH

LESSON 12
YEARS 7–10

Past reactions to loss

▶ Objective

At the end of the lesson the students will be able:

- to identify their past reactions to loss by asking their parents to recall how they (the students) reacted to a particular event.

▶ Content

Ask the class to interview their parents about how they — the students — reacted as children when pets died (or possibly family members and relatives). Remind the students that their parents may find it difficult to talk about previous deaths and losses, because they may still have strong feelings about some aspects of them. Encourage the students to use the exercise to explain to their parents some of the positive things they have experienced in doing these activities in class.

Suggested questions

When did I hear about death?
How did I react emotionally?
What was I told about death?
Was I involved in any rituals surrounding the death, e.g. did I hold a
    funeral for my pet or attend the funeral of a relative?
Did I do anything out of character in the days or weeks after the death?
Did I talk about death, ask questions, etc.?

▶ Conclusion

Students report back to the class on their findings and complete the following sentences which they can share with the class.

The most interesting thing I learnt from the discussion with my parents was...

After my talk with my parents I felt...

UNIT 2: THE IMPACT OF DEATH

LESSON 13
YEARS 9–12

The media's coverage of death

▶ Objective

At the end of the lesson the students will be able:
- to identify the concept of death as portrayed in the media.

▶ Content

Explain to the class that in terms of news and current affairs, telecommunication developments have resulted in almost eyewitness experience of wars and disasters for viewers. Additionally, regular television programs, particularly the 'soapies', handle death and loss. Divide the class into groups. Each student is given a copy of Worksheet 7. For homework they are to watch the particular television program or news coverage allocated to their group and record the manner in which death is handled and talked about.

In their groups, students share their findings and write three or four sentences that draw together their results. These should be shared with the class.

Again in their groups, the students are given copies of different daily newspapers. Excluding the 'Funerals' and 'In Memoriam' sections, the students are to collect the following information:

---

1. How many column centimetres are devoted to stories involving death?
2. What are the circumstances of the death referred to, e.g., war, murder, fire, illness?
3. What age are the persons involved? (You may have to estimate.)
4. What type of language is used to describe the death, e.g., factual, emotive?
5. In each of the stories is there any reporting of how other people reacted? If so, what is reported?

UNIT 2: THE IMPACT OF DEATH

▶ Conclusion

Each group reports its findings.

As a class the following summary statements should be completed. After you have written them on the board or overhead, allow time for reflection and then begin the class discussion of them.

1. Most of the newspaper reports about death involve...
2. The newspaper coverage of people's reaction to death is...
3. Thus the coverage of death by the media is...

▶ Extension Activities

1. The class as a group writes a letter to the newspaper editors and producers of local television news and dramas reporting its findings and making suggestions as to how the media could reflect accurately people's experience of death.
2. The Australian Broadcasting Tribunal has no standards that directly relate to the intrusion into grief. Using the information on Worksheet 8, the class can monitor television news coverage of a sudden death or disaster.

    With this information have them write to the producer of the television news program or the Australian Broadcasting Tribunal, reporting their findings. If they believe the coverage was appropriate they are to say why; if they believe the coverage contained elements against the ABC guidelines (given on Worksheet 8), they are to describe the problem areas.

Worksheet 7

> ▸ *Instructions*

One group is to watch an edition of the nightly news; another an episode of a police drama; the third an episode of a medically-oriented drama.

The media's coverage of death

Program	
Incident	
Spoken (by whom) or visual (describe scene)	
What was the age of the person/s who had died?	
Circumstances of the death? Realistic?	
If spoken reference, what was the speaker's attitude?	
How did other people react? Was the reality of death accepted?	
Did the incident portray the concept of 'good being rewarded and evil being punished'?	

The Australian Journalists' Association *Code of Ethics (9)* states that journalists: 'shall respect private grief and personal privacy and shall have the right to resist the compulsion to intrude.'

The ABC *Editorial and Program Practices in Radio and Television* (October 1989) state that:

'7.8.1. The decision whether to broadcast certain pictures or sounds should be based on the normal judgment of their newsworthiness and reporting value, together with a proper regard for the reasonable susceptibilities of audiences to detail of what is broadcast. A terrorist massacre at an airport is an example of an event which may have to be reported, but reports should never linger on corpses or the sufferings of the wounded. Wide shots of the dead may be necessary to make a point, perhaps to show the risk of disease or the problems facing the rescue workers: unnecessary close-ups should be avoided.

'7.8.2 Violent events should never be sensationalised or presented for their own sake. A difficult balance needs to be struck between the inherent strength of the images and proper detachment... A deliberate decision to shock should be the result only of the most careful consideration of the potential consequences and of the reaction from the audience. Particular sequences or programs may require some announcement, before they begin, that the material may be distressing to some viewers or listeners.'

The Australian Broadcasting Tribunal in the 'Inquiry into Violence on Television' (December 1988) reported that the viewers believed some reporting was lacking in good taste.

'One item that gained near universal disapproval was the harassment of a distressed survivor of the Queen Street incident. Here a young woman was pursued by a news team asking questions even though she said she did not want to talk about the incident. "To stick the b... camera up someone's nose when she's just had her friends killed — no consideration for them at all".' (ABT 1989 p. 23)

A 1985 survey in the United States reported that two-thirds of the people interviewed believed that the journalists had taken advantage of the victims. The television camera 'zooms in on the face of a dead person's relative — and stays there as the face dissolves into grief'. (Zuckerman & Whitaker, 1989, quoted in D. Powell, *Television Intrusion into the Privacy of Bereavement*, ABC News and Current Affairs, March, 1990.)

From reading this information and watching television coverage of grief and loss I conclude that ....

....

....

....

UNIT 2: THE IMPACT OF DEATH

▶ **LESSON 14**
YEARS 10-12

The creative impetus of death

▶ *Objectives*

At the end of the lesson the students will:

- evaluate the creative potential of loss experiences through their own research;
- explore the theme of death as portrayed in works of art.

▶ *Content*

Divide the class into two groups. Each group then divides into smaller groups to research and report back on the following topics:

1. 'The experience of the death of someone close has been the impetus to the creation of many great works of art.'
    Test this supposition by carrying out some research into the circumstances surrounding the composition of well-known musical, literary and other artistic works.
2. 'The powerful feelings that death and loss can evoke are reflected in the themes of many great works of art'.
    Test this supposition by establishing some common themes found in art, literature and music, e.g., love, war/conflict, death and loss. By surveying people or their own analysis of works, establish the validity of this statement.

Useful references:

R.A. Pacholski, 'Death Themes in Music', *Death Studies*, Vol. 10, No. 3, 1986, pp. 239-63.

R.A. Pacholski, 'Death Themes in the Visual Arts', *Death Studies*, Vol. 10, No. 1, 1986, pp. 59-74.

Unit 2: The Impact of Death

LESSON 15
YEARS 7-10

The disposal of pets

▶ Objective

At the end of the lesson the students will have:

- investigated the disposal of family pets.

▶ Content

Divide the class into groups.

From the classified telephone directory find out how many companies are involved in the disposal of pets. Allocate one company per pair of students. They conduct a telephone interview, asking the following questions:

1. How are pets disposed of?
2. What is the cost?
3. Are there plaques or headstones marking where the remains are?
4. What do people write on the plaques/headstones?
5. How many animals are disposed of in a month?
6. Are there mainly cats and dogs disposed of or are there other animals as well?

Other group activities:

1. The students investigate how other cultures have disposed of animals, e.g., Egyptians (cats), Hindus (cows).
2. A pair of students interview a taxidermist, asking the following questions:
    a. Does he/she ever stuff dead pets for their owners?
    b. What would be the cost to preserve a family cat?
    c. How is taxidermy done?
3. Students investigate 'rich' pets, that is, those who have been left money in their owners' wills. What provisions have been made for these animals?
4. Students investigate heroic deeds by and memorials to animals.
5. A pair of students interview the local health inspector to find out what regulations might apply to burying your pet in your backyard.

UNIT 2: THE IMPACT OF DEATH

▶ *Conclusion*

The students report back on their group activity and then individually complete the following sentence:

If my pet were to die I would ....
....
....
....
....

UNIT 2: THE IMPACT OF DEATH

LESSON 16
YEARS 7-10

Responding to death

▶ Objective

At the end of the lesson the students will:
- have identified some emotional responses to death.

▶ Content

Introduce the lesson by recalling the discussions from previous lessons on the type of experiences we can have that result in a grief response. Hand out Worksheet 9. Read the excerpt from Charles Dickens' *David Copperfield*, where David learns of the death of his mother.

▶ Conclusion

If David were a friend of yours, what would you do when you heard the news of his mother's death? How would you support David in his grief?

Worksheet 9

1 'A mist rose between Mrs Creakle and me, and her figure
2 seemed to move in it for an instant. Then I felt the
3 burning tears run down my face and it was steady again.
4 "She is dangerously ill", she added. I knew all now.
5 "She is dead".
6   There was no need to tell me so. I had already broken
7 down into a desolate cry and felt an orphan in the wide
8 world.
9   She was very kind to me. She kept me there all day,
10 and left me alone sometimes; and I cried and wore myself
11 to sleep, and awoke and cried again. When I could cry no
12 more, I began to think, and then the oppression on my
13 chest was heaviest and my grief a dull pain, that there
14 was no ease for.
15   And yet my thoughts were idle; not intent on the
16 calamity that weighed upon my heart, but idly loitering
17 near it. I thought of our house shut up and hushed. I
18 thought of the little baby who Mrs Creakle said had been
19 pining away for some time and who they believed would die
20 too. I thought of my father's grave in the churchyard by
21 our house and of my mother lying there beneath the tree I
22 knew so well.
23   I stood upon a chair when I was left alone and looked
24 into the glass to see how red my eyes were, and how
25 sorrowful my face. I considered after some hours were
26 gone, if my tears were really hard to flow now, as they
27 seemed to be, what, in connexion with my loss, it would
28 affect me most to think of when I drew near home — for I
29 was going home for the funeral. I am sensible of having
30 felt that dignity attached to me among the rest of the
31 boys and that I was important in my affliction.'

from Charles Dickens' *David Copperfield*

Discuss:
1. What emotion/s is David feeling?
   a. at lines 1 and 2
   b. 6 and 7
   c. 10 and 11
   d. 12, 13, and 14
   e. the last sentence
2. What do you think about David looking at himself in the mirror to see how red his eyes were and how sorrowful his face?
3. Does David have some ideas about how he should be behaving when grieving? Where do people get ideas about how they should grieve? How do *you* think they should behave? (Recall discussions about individual reactions to loss.)

UNIT 2: THE IMPACT OF DEATH

LESSON 17
YEARS 7-10

Funerals and burial practices

▶ Objectives

At the end of this lesson the students will have:

- researched the funeral and burial practices of at least one country;
- contributed to the compilation of a class wall chart identifying funeral practices around the world.

▶ Content

Ask the class, 'How many have been to a funeral service in a church, at a crematorium or at a graveside? Has anyone been to a service in another country?' If so, get them to recall what happened. Tell the class that funeral and burial customs reflect the culture and religion of the society in which they occur.

Distribute Worksheet 10. If the class has students from many cultures complete the Worksheet from that orientation, e.g. an Italian funeral in Australia. If there are only a few of non Anglo-Celtic origin the worksheet can be completed by research.

For homework the students, in pairs, are to find out the information on their nominated country/culture, e.g., Jewish, Japanese, Aboriginal, Indian. This information is to be transferred to sheets of newsprint in the next lesson to form a frieze around the room. Students can add any illustrations they have found relating to their particular area of research.

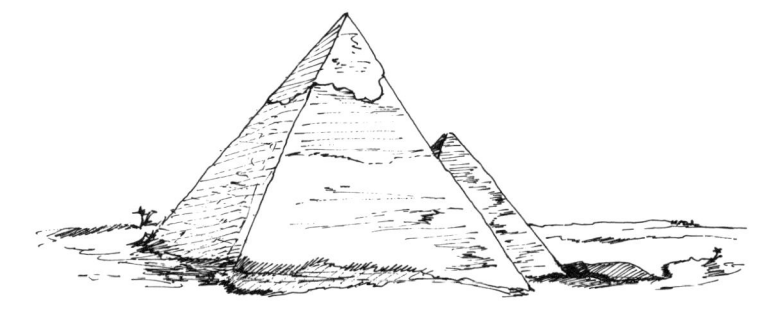

Philippines coffin, Ifugao tribe.   The pyramids of Egypt

Worksheet 10

Custom/Practice	Country/Culture: ....
How is the body prepared for burial?	
How do friends and family express their sympathy?	
What type of service is held to remember the dead?	
How is the body disposed of?	

UNIT 3: EXPLORING YOUR OWN DEATH

LESSON 18
YEARS 7-10

Past, present and future

▶ Objectives

At the end of this lesson the students will have:
- identified predictable changes in their physical development;
- identified predictable changes in their social world.

▶ Content

Introduce the topic by saying, 'Today we are going to look at some aspect of our lives as they were in the past, are currently and how we imagine them to be in the future.' Distribute Worksheet 11, and ask the class to complete it as best they can, by themselves.

When most of the students are finished ask them to write a few sentences on the major changes in their appearance in the past ten years and in their relationships with their family and friends. Ask for volunteers to share this. Then ask the class to focus on what they have written about their appearance and social life for when they are 70. How many have mentioned something about being young for their age, or have words to suggest stereotyping of elderly people, e.g., grey hair, bald, glasses, walking stick? Why do you think you will appear young for your age? Is it a fear of age and death?

UNIT 3: EXPLORING YOUR OWN DEATH

Why do you think you have an image of elderly people as grey and frail? Is there anything you can do about your life now that may alter your physical appearance in the future? From the students' responses to the worksheet, compile a list on the board of 'How I can expect my social life to change in the future?'.

▸ Conclusion

Review this list with the class. Point out that these changes in our physical appearance and social lives can be anticipated, just as we know that some day we will all die.

"ME" at various ages

	5 years	15 years	45 years	70 years
What is your hair like?				
What is your body like?				
Do you wear glasses, hearing aid, etc.?				
Who are your close friends?				
Are both your parents alive and living with you?				
What is the happiest memory you have?				
What is the saddest memory you have?				

▼ Worksheet 11

Read and discuss the following poem.

A Crabbit Old Woman

What do you see, nurses, what do you see?
Are you thinking when you look at me —
A crabbit old woman, not very wise,
Uncertain of habit, with far away eyes,
Who dribbles her food, and makes no reply
When you say in a loud voice, 'I do wish you'd try!'
Who seems not to notice the things that you do,
And forever is losing a stocking or shoe.
Who, unresisting or not, lets you do as you will, with
Bathing and feeding the long day to fill.
Is that what you are thinking? Is that what you see?
Then open your eyes, nurse, you're looking at me.
I tell you I am as I sit here so still,
As I use at your bidding, as I eat at your will,
I'm a small child often with a father and mother,
Brothers and sisters who love one another.
A young girl of sixteen, with wings on her feet,
Dreaming that soon now a lover I'll meet.
A bride soon a-twenty, my heart gives a leap,
Remembering the vows that I promised to keep;
At twenty-five now I have young of my own,
Who need me to build a secure, happy home;
A woman of thirty, my own now grow fast,
Bound to each other with ties that should last.
At forty, my young sons have grown and gone,
But my man's beside me to see I don't mourn.
At fifty, once more babies play round my knee,
Again we know children, my loved one and me.
Dark days are upon me, my husband is dead,
I look to the future, I shudder with dread,
For my young are all rearing young of their own,
And I think of the years and the love that I've known.
I'm now an old woman and nature is cruel —
'Tis jest to make old age look like a fool.
The body it crumbles, grace and vigour depart,
There now is a stone where once I had a heart.
But inside this old carcass a young girl still dwells,
And now and again my battered heart swells,
I remember the joys, I remember the pain,
And I'm loving and living life over again.
I think of the years all too few gone too fast,
And accept the stark fact that nothing can last.
So open your eyes, nurses, open and see,
Not a crabbit old woman, look closer...

See me!

(Anonymous)

UNIT 3: EXPLORING YOUR OWN DEATH

LESSON 19
YEARS 10-12

EXTENSION LESSON

The changes that can be expected in later life

▶ Objective

At the end of the lesson the students will have:
- researched the possible physical and social changes they may experience later in their lifespan.

▶ Content

By interview and research the students find out what changes occur with aging. Write the following on the board or overhead.

Research Questions

physiologically — what organs deteriorate? what skin changes occur? does alcohol affect you the same way as when you are younger, etc.?

sexually — do older people stop having intercourse? is it the same or different from when they are younger? do men stop producing sperm, etc.?

socially — do older people like the company of people their own age or younger? how do older people feel when their circle of friends gets smaller as they all die?

intellectually — do older people lose intelligence as they age? do older people lose their memory?

UNIT 3: EXPLORING YOUR OWN DEATH

▶ **LESSON 20**
YEARS 7-10

Living life now

▶ *Objective*

At the end of the lesson the students will have:
- contemplated their death and its impact on the life they are now living.

▶ *Content*

Indicate to the class, 'As a follow on from previous lessons, today we are going to look at our own lives and in doing so think about our own death.' Educators in Australia and overseas have found that thinking about death gives you a greater appreciation of life and rather than being a morbid and sad topic they have found it actually encourages people to adopt a lifestyle that is more positive and fulfilling.

▶ *Development activity**

Ask the class to think about some of the people they most enjoyed spending time with in the past month. List 10 of them.

Then have them think of five people they would like to spend time with, and write down their names (people not already on their list).

After allowing sufficient time, give them the following instructions:

1. Write O next to anyone older than 60.
2. Write Y next to anyone younger than 10.
3. Place a D next to the people who are most likely to die first.
4. Place a T next to those people you feel you are able to talk to about problems.
5. Think of four things you own that are special to you, then place a P next to the people you would give these prized possessions to if you knew you were dying.

UNIT 3: EXPLORING YOUR OWN DEATH

After students have completed the sheet, ask them the following questions:
1. Has the activity identified some people you would like to spend more time with or people you would like to add to your list?
2. Do you have people of all ages on your list?
3. Do you think people on your list would guess that you had included them on the list? Would you tell them about this?
4. Looking at the people you have identified as most likely to die first, are they all older people? Would you like to change the amount of time you spend with any of the people on your list?

▶ Conclusion

Have the students complete this sentence:

As a result of this exercise I intend to ....

If time permits, ask the students if any would like to share their completed sentences.

* adapted from J. Greenberg, *Student-centered Health Instruction*, Addison Wesley, Reading, Massachusetts, 1978.

UNIT 3: EXPLORING YOUR OWN DEATH

LESSON 21
YEARS 7-10

Own death awareness

▶ Objective

At the end of the lesson the students will have:
- begun to examine some of their concerns about their own mortality.

▶ Content

Refer to previous lessons on people's fear about death. 'Sometimes this fear relates to losing those we love, sometimes it relates to fear about our own death. Today we are going to look at our concerns about our own death.' Hand out Worksheet 13.

Have students discuss the worksheet in small groups. Then ask the class as a whole, 'What do you think acceptance of your own death would involve? Let's list some things on the board that you think would indicate acceptance of one's own death sometime in the future.' (Responses could include: being able to talk about death, expressing their love for friends and relatives, accepting their own limitations.)

▶ Conclusion

Students complete the following sentence and, if they desire, share with their group or the whole class.

As a result of doing this exercise I intend to...

Concerns about our own death questionnaire

Circle the response that most suits your current beliefs. For questions 2, 4, 6, 8, you may circle more than one response.

1. How often do you think about your own death?
   a. Very frequently (at least once a day)
   b. Frequently
   c. Occasionally
   d. Rarely (no more than once a year)
   e. Very rarely or never
2. Has there been a time in your life when you wanted to die?
   a. Yes, mainly because of great physical pain
   b. Yes, mainly because of great emotional pain
   c. Yes, mainly to escape an intolerable social or interpersonal situation
   d. Yes, mainly because of great embarrassment
   e. Yes, for a reason other than the above
   f. No
3. What is your belief about the cause of most deaths?
   a. Most deaths result directly from the conscious efforts of the people who die
   b. Most deaths have strong components of conscious and unconscious participation by the persons who die
   c. Most deaths just happen, they are caused by events over which individuals have no control
   d. Other (specify) ....
4. When you think of your own death — or when circumstances make you realise your own mortality — how do you feel?
   a. fearful
   b. discouraged
   c. depressed
   d. purposeless
   e. resolved because of its inevitability
   f. pleasure, in being alive
   g. Other (specify) ....
   ....
5. How often have you been in the situation in which you seriously thought you might die?
   a. many times
   b. several times
   c. once or twice
   d. never
6. For whom or what, might you be willing to sacrifice your life?
   a. for a loved one
   b. for an idea or a moral principle
   c. in combat or a grave emergency where a life could be saved
   d. not for any reason
7. If your doctor knew that you had a terminal disease and a limited time to live, would you want him/her to tell you?
   a. yes
   b. no
   c. it would depend on the circumstances

▼ worksheet 13*

8. Which of the following has influenced your present attitude to death the most?
   a. pollution of the environment
   b. domestic violence
   c. television
   d. wars
   e. the possibility of a nuclear war
   f. poverty
   g. the way someone close to me died
   h. my parents' view
   i. my religious views
   j. what I have learnt from reading/others
   k. other (specify) ....
9. What efforts do you believe should be made to keep you alive?
   a. all possible efforts — transplantations, kidney dialysis, etc.
   b. efforts reasonable to my condition
   c. where the quality of life is questionable, I should be permitted to die
10. If it were entirely up to you, how would you want your body disposed of after you die.
    a. burial
    b. cremation and ashes stored in memorial wall
    c. donation to medical school or science
    d. cremation and ashes disposed of as I request
    e. don't care, I'm indifferent to this

* Adapted from E.S. Shneidman, 'Death Questionnaire', *Psychology Today*, Communications Research Machines Inc., 1972.

UNIT 3: EXPLORING YOUR OWN DEATH

LESSON 22
YEARS 10-12

Being at your own funeral

▸ Objective

At the end of the lesson students will have:
- imagined their own funeral through guided imagery.

▸ Content

Conduct a relaxation activity with the class, such as deep breathing or progressive muscle relaxation (see B. Montgomery & L. Evans, *You and Stress*, in resources list).

When this has finished and while students still have their eyes closed, say, 'We are going to follow that activity with a similar one that relates to the topic we have been studying recently.

> I want you to imagine your own funeral. Visualise how you are lying in the coffin.
> People are coming to see you. Who are they? What are they doing? How are they feeling?
> What are they saying to each other?
> Do they speak to you? If so, what do they say?
> What would you wish you could say to them?
> How are you feeling?

'Open your eyes. On a piece of paper describe your funeral, either by writing about it or doing a series of drawings of it and using bubbles coming from people indicating their thoughts and feelings.' (Adapted from Jeffrey Schrank, *Teaching Human Beings: 101 Subversive Activities of the Classroom*, Boston, Beacon Press, 1972.)

UNIT 4: GRIEF SUPPORT

LESSON 23
YEARS 7-10

Qualities of a supportive friend

▶ Objectives

By the end of this lesson the students will have:

- identified strategies they can employ that may help support a grieving friend or family member;
- identified statements and behaviours that may not be supportive to grieving people.

▶ Content

Introduce the topic by saying, 'Today we are going to try to develop skills in being a supportive friend or family member to those who are grieving. Two of the difficult things involved in this are that people who are grieving may reject your support. Also while you may want to make things better for the person, you need to accept that you can't take their pain away. People, children included, need the opportunity to "feel" their feelings, not be talked out of them. You need to understand and accept the painful feelings they are experiencing. If a person tells you to go away, they are telling you they want privacy. Give them that privacy. Say "I understand you want to be alone, I am available if you want me".'

Ask the class to recall a time when they were feeling sad. Can you remember anything people said or did that you feel did/did not help?

Compile a list on the board, under the headings:

        Helpful things   Unhelpful things

Remind students that we are all individuals and what might help one person might not help another. But there are some general things that are likely to block people's expression of feelings or pass judgment on their behaviour.

Show an overhead with the following information:

	Example
Passing judgment on behaviour	She didn't seem to cry very much
Passing judgment on feelings	I don't think you should feel guilty; there was nothing you could do
Blocking feelings	Buck up, it could have been worse

UNIT 4: GRIEF SUPPORT

Conclude by saying: There are many ways you can help people: by doing things for them, by listening to them, by accepting their feelings.

Read pages 77–82 of *You Take the High Road* by Mary Pershall (Penguin Plus, 1988). The book tells the story of a teenager, Sam, whose baby brother Nickie dies. This part of the story recounts Sam's first meeting with her friend Liz since the death. After reading the story ask the class to recall some of the ways Sam described her feelings. What does she want Liz to do? How is Liz supportive?

If time permits read additional pages 116–17. What is the teacher doing to be supportive? What is Liz doing? After five months is Sam over her brother's death?

Grieving people may not be able to identify things that you can do to help. There are different kinds of support:

- informational support, e.g., what happens at a funeral, what clothes people usually wear;
- emotional support, e.g., asking them to tell you about their loss;
- practical support, e.g., cooking meals, taking the dog for a walk;
- social support, e.g., providing a sense of belonging by inclusion in activities.

Ask the class to think of things they can do to be supportive:

- to a friend. (Some suggestions might include: ask them over to watch television, listen to music or go for a walk; ask them to go shopping with you to buy a new tape.)
- to adults, e.g., a grandparent or a neighbour. (Some suggestions here might include: prepare a meal or some home-cooked biscuits; go to the supermarket for them; take care of the children for the day; walk the dog for them; mow the lawn or weed the garden; address envelopes for the 'thank you for your sympathy' cards; vacuum the house; write to their out-of-town friends and acquaintances who do not yet know of the death.)

You might also suggest that if people seem reluctant to verbalise acceptance of support, they can be given a card to be sent when they want contact. Put this sample card on the board or overhead:

_____ I will come for coffee on _____ at _____.

_____ I won't be able to come over.

_____ I need to be left alone for a while.

_____ Other _____

UNIT 4: GRIEF SUPPORT

LESSON 24
YEARS 7-10

Using people for support

▶ Objectives

At the end of the lesson the students will have:
- explored the characteristics of their supportive relationships;
- identified their own support networks.

▶ Content

Explain that one of the most significant factors that researchers have discovered that helps a grieving person is the existence and use of support systems. What is a support system? Some young people have the belief that to be grown up and independent you must cope with problems on your own, that if you turn to others for help, you will be seen as not being independent. This belief may result in your suppressing many feelings. You may also have the belief that after a short period of time, you should no longer share feelings with support persons because you will be putting too much strain on friendships.

What is your support network like?

Ask the students to take a sheet of paper and draw a circle in the centre of it. Write 'self' in the middle. Then ask the class to imagine they have a relationship problem; it may be a conflict with parents, a brother or sister, a boyfriend/girlfriend. They are to think about the people they could talk to about this. Those they are most likely to talk to are to be put close to their circle. Those they are less likely to talk to are to be put further away. If they feel the person would let them talk freely, a strong line can connect the two; if they don't feel totally comfortable talking to that person, a dotted line can be used.

There are a number of problems we experience in giving and receiving support. Ask the class to think of a time when in offering or receiving support problems occurred. Draw up a list on the board or overhead transparency:

Problems in giving support	Problems in receiving support
e.g. may not have the skill	may believe you have to cope yourself
support is rejected	do not trust others

UNIT 4: GRIEF SUPPORT

Ask the class how support can help. Draw up a list.

> Support can help by providing:
>
> people who will listen;
> the opportunity to share the loss and maybe lighten the burden of the feelings;
> the opportunity to develop new relationships to replace those that have ended;
> the opportunity to recall memories of the person or object that has been lost;
> the comforting physical presence of another person at a time when someone is feeling lonely.

Have the students complete Worksheet 14.

▶ Conclusion

Ask the class to individually look at their list and consider carefully what they have written. Give them a few minutes to consider the following questions: Can they add any names? Do different people provide different support? Are there some things they can change about their giving and receiving of support behaviour?

Worksheet 14

My supportive relationships

1. The person I most enjoy being with is ....
2. I feel closest to ....
3. I am most likely to share my problems with ....
4. I am most likely to be comforted by ....
5. The things that might stop me sharing problems with others are ....
   ....
6. What I can do to be supportive to others is ....
7. I think I actually am supportive as follows:

to (people):	in these ways:

Complete the sentence:
Some things I could change about giving and/or receiving support are ....
....
....
....

UNIT 4: GRIEF SUPPORT

▶ LESSON 25
YEARS 7–10

Being supportive

▶ *Objectives*

At the end of the lesson the students will be able:

- to list ways of coping with loss experiences;
- to state strategies for helping a grieving friend and have practised these in a role-play.

Remind the class of a previous lesson (Lesson 23) and the things in *You Take the High Road* that Liz did to help Sam. Ask the class in groups to come up with a list of ways they have coped with 'little deaths', that is, disappointments, failures, unexpected changes in life. Share these as a class or present students with the following list and ask them to recall which ones they used.

Talked to others, talked it through by myself, cried, took heart from support of friends, accepted it as time passed, kept busy, developed new relationships, drew on family support and wrote about my feelings, philosophical/religious beliefs.

Collate the students' responses.

How do you hope other people will respond when you share your feelings with them? (It is possible that the males in the class may have difficulty accepting the expression of feelings as legitimate.)

Ask the students to imagine now that a grieving friend has come to them for help. Describe to the students the following ideas about how they can help.

Openness	to what the person is saying, leave your beliefs behind
Listening	without talking
Presence	being there when needed
Acceptance	of the person's feelings, no matter how odd they may appear
Self	encouraging self-sufficiency, that is, behaviour that will restore self-esteem.

Unit 4: Grief Support

The students, in pairs, could role-play some of the 'little deaths' they identified earlier in the lesson. Each person in turn could be the grieving person, with their partner practising OLPAS (openness, listening, presence, acceptance and self).

(The students should be given the opportunity to 'pass' on presenting an experience they have had and be given permission to create an imaginary experience.)

▶ Conclusion

If you are the grieving person what is your responsibility in terms of talking to others? (Responses could include such things as: being prepared to share feelings, not expecting the other person to solve my problem.) Conclude by telling the class that this type of help given to others and being helped in this way is 'interdependence' between people, not dependence.

UNIT 4: GRIEF SUPPORT

LESSON 26
YEARS 7-10

Helping grieving adolescents

▸ Objectives

At the end of the lesson the students will:
- have identified the needs of some adolescents who have experienced losses;
- be able to describe the reactions of some adolescents to their loss.

▸ Content

Tell the class that as a follow-on from the last lesson, they are going to see a video about some Australian adolescents who have experienced major losses in their lives. Distribute Worksheet 15.

Divide the class into groups. Allocate one or more characters in the video to each group. They are to listen carefully to what is in the film about each of these characters and then report to the class on:

1. the character's emotional response to the loss
2. how the character coped with the loss
3. if the character were a friend, how could the students be supportive?

Show the video *A Bolt from the Blue* (South Australian Film Corporation, 21 minutes).

▸ Conclusion

Each group reports back. If time permits replay part of the video.

Worksheet 15

Characters in *A Bolt from the Blue*

In groups discuss and report on:
1. The character's emotional response to the loss
2. How the character coped with the loss
3. If the character were a friend, how could you be supportive?

> Kyralie is a Year 8 high school student, who was struck by a car on a pedestrian crossing when she was in 6th class. She has a broken spine and a paralysed diaphragm.

> Rick is now aged 20. He was injured in a motor cycle accident on his country property when he was 18. He suffered brain damage and spent months in hospital. He is now able to walk, but his speech is difficult to understand.

> Andrew is in Year 8. His mother died after a long illness suffering from muscular dystrophy. Andrew's father kept telling Andrew his mother was getting better, but he had heard the community nurse say she was dying. Shortly after his mother's death, his father also died. He now lives with an older brother and his girlfriend.

> Troy is in Year 9. He was diagnosed with a brain tumour at age 14. As a result of chemotherapy Troy lost all his hair and wore a wig till it regrew.

> George (female) is in Year 11. Her uncle and cousin died in the Ash Wednesday bush fires. Her uncle was burnt to death when he was trapped by the property fence. The cousin died while trying to rescue neighbours.

Adapted from Student Welfare Co-ordination Program (1991) Grief and Loss Workshop: *Living with Loss*. Leader's Materials. Department of School Education, South Coast Region, Wollongong, NSW.

UNIT 4: GRIEF SUPPORT

LESSON 27
YEARS 7-10

Saying goodbye

▶ Objectives

At the end of the lesson the students will have:

- identified and practised ways of consoling a grieving friend;
- written a letter saying goodbye to a friend who is moving house.

▶ Content

Tell the class, 'We all experience times of rapid change in our social worlds; people move in and out of our lives. We need to be able to say goodbye to people who are, or have been, important to us, e.g., when someone moves house, dies, a change in friendship, a broken love affair.' Divide the class into similar groups to the previous lessons. The students are asked to share with the group a time when someone close moved schools, houses or went away. (Stress that this sharing is voluntary.) Ask those willing to describe what their chosen event meant to them. Ask pupils to finish any unfinished goodbyes by sending the person who has left an imaginary telegram with a message such as

I want you to know ....
I never told you ....

Ask the class to recall information from a previous lesson on ways to help a grieving friend (openness, listening, presence, acceptance and self).

In triads drawn from the groups one person is to describe a loss they have experienced or an imaginary one (e.g. missing out on being selected for a state team because of an injury), one other person is to console them, the third person is to observe. An imaginary scenario could also be used, e.g., tell an 8-year-old brother about the death of a pet. The observer is not to participate, but is to give feedback at the end as to what he or she saw. (Not to comment on personal characteristics or performance.) You could ask, 'Did both people look comfortable about what they were saying?'

UNIT 4: GRIEF SUPPORT

▶ *Conclusion*

Write a letter to an older person, e.g., grandparent or neighbour, consoling them on a recent death, using some of the principles above. (This could be in the form of a verse that could be added to the sympathy card designed in an earlier lesson.) These letters are returned for redistribution to the class and replies are written. Then ask for some students to read out their letters and their replies.

▶ *Section 2*

YEARS 11-12

UNIT 5: LOSS AND GRIEF

LESSON 28
YEARS 11-12

Loss: a universal human experience

▶ Objective

At the end of this lesson the student will be able:
- to describe the categories of loss.

Useful reference: Bertha J. Simons, *A Time to Grieve: Loss as a universal human experience*, New York, Family Service Association of America, 1979.

▶ Content

In order for students to understand the categories of loss, they need to be aware of the changes in their own lives and how feelings of loss accompany these changes.

On the board or on an overhead transparency write the following heading:

CHANGE = LOSS = GRIEF = BEHAVIOUR

Ask the students to work in small groups of approximately 8 to 10 and list the changes that have occurred in their lives.

Each group can write their list of changes on butcher's paper or on an overhead transparency.

Allow about 10 minutes for this activity.

When completed ask for one person from each group to read out their list. To save time and repetition after the first group has read their list, ask the other groups to add those changes not previously mentioned.

Once the students have given their lists you may wish to compare their changes with those listed in the Categories of Loss which Bertha Simons developed:

Unit 5: Loss and Grief

Categories of loss

Loss has been grouped into four major categories:
1. THE LOSS OF A SIGNIFICANT PERSON
2. THE LOSS OF A PART OF THE SELF
3. THE LOSS OF EXTERNAL OBJECTS
4. DEVELOPMENTAL LOSS

Whilst these losses are listed in the various categories, there is considerable overlap and one loss often impinges on another; as a result the distinctions between categories tend to blur.

1. *Loss of a significant person.*
   Death of a loved one — the ultimate loss, final and complete; also desertion, separation, divorce, abortion, stillbirth.
2. *Loss of a part of the self.*
   a) Physical
   - Structural
   - Functional

   Structural loss: loss of a limb, loss of an organ, disfigurement, loss of hair, loss of teeth, any outward change, loss of body-image (through surgery, burns, accident).
   Functional: loss through stroke, paralysis, deafness, blindness, arthritis, infertility.
   b) Psychological: loss of memory, judgment, pride, control, status, usefulness, independence, esteem, values, ideals.
   c) Social: loss of roles, employment, friends; geographic moves, travel.
   d) Community and cultural: loss through immigration, urban renewal, refugee experience.
3. *Loss of external objects.*
   Loss of possessions — money, jewels, property, and 'symbols of identity' such as photographs, artefacts, etc, through burglary, robbery, and natural disasters such as fire and floods.
4. *Developmental loss.*
   Birth trauma, weaning, growing up, school, exam failures, school-to-work transition, leaving home, new relationships, marriage, old age, multiple cumulative losses.

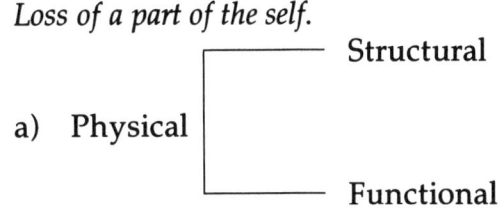

Unit 5: Loss and Grief

These four categories will provide the basis of some of the work you will be doing in the next few weeks as you explore the way in which people respond to these kinds of losses.

Reform the groups. Ask the students to now try and think of the feelings associated with those changes. Again make a list of the feelings. In this part of the lesson it is important to realise that not all the feelings listed will necessarily be negative.

Once this has been completed, choose a different group and ask their spokesperson to report on the list of feelings they have written down. Add to this list from the other groups. Briefly discuss the range of feelings expressed; look for similarities, differences between groups, gender differences, etc. At this point it is necessary to draw attention to the positive feelings expressed and recognise that good feelings tend not to cause us a problem. We do not get upset or seek help because we are happy! Delete the positive feelings from the list and you are left with a list of negative feelings. Refer back to the heading on the board, Change = Loss = Grief = Behaviour. What we now have listed on these sheets are what we can describe as grief reactions and we will explore these next time.

▶ Conclusion

Ask the students to work on the Holmes-Rahe Survey of Recent Experiences (Worksheet 16) at home with their parents and bring their responses to the next lesson.

The aim of the exercise is to try to establish how much change has occurred in the families of the students. It may help the student and perhaps the family as a whole to recognise that if there have been a significant number of changes or life events, there could be some hitherto unrecognised grief.

Worksheet 16

The Holmes-Rahe Survey of recent experiences*

Read each of the events listed below, and circle the number next to any event which has occurred in your life recently. There are no right or wrong answers. The aim is just to help identify which of these events you have experienced lately. A recent event is one which you think is still affecting you.

Life events	Life change units (LCUs)
Death of a spouse	100
Divorce	73
Marital separation	65
Jail term	63
Death of close family member	63
Personal injury or illness	53
Fired at work	47
Marital reconciliation	45
Retirement	45
Change in health of family member	44
Pregnancy	40
Sex difficulties	39
Gain of new family member	30
Business readjustment	39
Change of financial state	38
Death of a close friend	37
Change to different line of work	36
Change in number of arguments with spouse	35
Mortgage over $30,000	31
Foreclosure of mortgage or loan	30
Change in responsibilities at work	29
Son or daughter leaving home	29
Trouble with in-laws	29
Outstanding personal achievement	28
Partner begins or stops work	26
Begin or end school	26
Change in living conditions	25
Revision of personal habits	24
Trouble with boss	23
Change in work hours or conditions	20
Change in residence	20
Change in schools	20
Change in recreation	19
Change in church activities	19
Change in social activities	18
Mortgage or loan less than $30,000	17
Change in sleeping habits	16
Change in number of family get-togethers	15
Change in eating habits	15
Vacation	13
Christmas	12
Minor violations of law	11

Now add up the numbers you have circled, to obtain your total life change units score.

* 'Holmes-Rahe Survey of Recent Experiences', *Journal of Psychosomatic Research*, Vol. 11, 1967, p. 31–2.

UNIT 5: LOSS AND GRIEF

LESSON 29
YEARS 11–12

Grief is normal

▶ Objective

At the end of this lesson the students will be able:

- to identify normal grief reactions.

A useful reference for this lesson: Bob Montgomery & Lynette Evans, *You and Stress*, (See resource list).

▶ Content

Write up on the board the same heading as for the last lesson,

CHANGE = LOSS = GRIEF = BEHAVIOUR.

Say to the students, 'You will recall last lesson we looked at the changes that you had experienced and identified the feelings of loss associated with those changes. When we remove the positive feelings, we had what we could describe, as a list of grief reactions. Look at the list again from the previous lesson.'

Ask the students what kinds of changes they were able to identify on the Holmes-Rahe Survey. In completing the questionnaire at home, did the family discuss their own personal reactions to change? What was their score? The Life Change Units give a score to each Life Event which when added together give an indication of the amount of stress a person is likely to experience. A score of 300 or more indicates that there is a high degree of stress; between 200 and 300, a reasonable degree of stress; 200 or below, a limited amount of stress. What is frequently forgotten is that stress is directly associated with loss and therefore grief. Graph the scores on the board if you wish.

The kind of change or loss the person has experienced will determine the degree of grief that person feels. A more significant loss, e.g., a close family member through death, will be more painful than a less significant one.

We have looked at the changes, described the feelings of loss associated with those changes and indicated that these feelings are grief reactions. We now need to consider what we do with these feelings.

The students are asked to think of those changes they contributed to the original list and the feelings associated with the change. Students write down what they did with those feelings or how they behaved. What kind of messages

UNIT 5: LOSS AND GRIEF

Sketch based on *The Scream* by Edvard Munch

did they receive from their families, etc.? Did they feel people understood them? What would they have liked people to say?

Ask the students to write down their responses to these kinds of questions or any other things that were significant to them at the time. Names should not be put on the sheets because they will be collected and collated so that we can see the range of reactions the class has had.

Remind the students that if they have become upset by thinking and talking about these things they should find someone with whom they can discuss it.

Use Worksheet 17 on Normal Grief Reactions so the students can see the range of reactions. For anyone who is disturbed by their own reactions, this list will provide a means of normalising their experience.

▶ Conclusion

Changes and loss often involve a crisis. In Chinese 'crisis' stands for danger and opportunity. Ask the class to identify any positive outcomes of their changes. You might also ask them to discover people who were able to use their 'crisis' or significant loss in a positive way. Refer to people like Helen Keller, or Harold S. Kushner who wrote the book *When Bad Things Happen to Good People,* or C.S. Lewis who wrote *A Grief Observed,* which has been made into a play and was on television under the title 'Shadowlands'. Another person they might research is Edvard Munch, a Norwegian artist who expressed his feelings about significant changes in his life through his paintings.

Normal grief reactions

EMOTIONS	Anxiety and fear
	Sadness
	Anger
	Guilt
	Inadequacy
	Hurt
	Relief
	Loneliness
PHYSICAL SENSATIONS	Hollowness in stomach
	Tightness in chest
	Tightness in throat
	Oversensitivity to noise
	A sense of depersonalisation
	Breathlessness, feeling short of breath
	Weakness of muscles
	Lack of energy
	Dry mouth
COGNITIONS	Disbelief
	Confusion
	Preoccupation
	Sense of presence
	Hallucinations
BEHAVIOURS	Sleep disturbances
	Appetite disturbances
	Absent-minded behaviour
	Social withdrawal
	Dreams of the deceased
	Avoiding reminders of the deceased
	Searching and calling out
	Sighing
	Restless overactivity
	Crying
	Visiting places and carrying objects that remind the survivor of the deceased
	Treasuring objects that belonged to the deceased

(Adapted from J.W. Worden, *Grief Counselling and Grief Therapy*, 2nd ed., Springer, New York, 1991.)

UNIT 6: THE IMPACT OF DEATH

LESSON 30
YEARS 11-12

Understanding loss in response to death

▶ Objectives

At the end of this lesson the students will:
- be able to describe the various modes of death;
- be able to identify the likely grief responses to expected and unexpected death.

▶ Content

Collect a whole range of material which helps the students gain an awareness of the different kinds of deaths that are reported. The material should include such things as: the death notices in the daily press, any major accidents, catastrophic events, war items, suicides, murders, children and adolescent deaths, reports of children who are dying, people with AIDS and other life-threatening illnesses.

Try and make the range of material as broad as possible. It may be appropriate to ask the students during the previous week to collect this material.

Question the students, 'Is there any way in which we could categorise these deaths?' Write on the board any suggestions they may make. Allow the discussion to be reasonably free but still focused on the categories and why they think they fit into these categories.

One way of categorisation is by Mode of Death:

    NATURAL   **ACCIDENTAL**   **SUICIDAL**   **HOMICIDAL**

Each of these kinds of deaths will bring quite different grief reactions. Place on an overhead the headings from the Determinants of Grief listed below. Allow the class to question and discuss these factors as the teacher is giving the information.

▶ Determinants of Grief

The Parkes and Weiss, *Harvard Bereavement Study* 1983, endeavoured to identify the likely ways in which people would respond to a major loss.

Unit 6: The Impact of Death

A number of factors will determine the person's response. Among these will be the age and stage in life cycle of the person who has died and of the grieving person. The study revealed the following factors:

1. **Who the person was** To predict how a person might respond to a major loss through death, we need to know the relationship the person had to the dead person, e.g., parent, child, grandparent, sibling, lover, friend etc.
2. **The nature of the attachment** How strong was the relationship or how attached were they to the deceased person?
    a) **strength of the attachment** How much did they love the person?
    b) **security of the attachment** To what extent was the deceased person important for their ongoing sense of security and self-esteem?
    c) **ambivalence of the relationship** While some degree of mixed feelings is normal in any relationship, if the negative feelings are stronger, the surviving person is likely to have more difficulty in resolving the grief.
    d) **conflicts with the deceased** Where a history of conflict has been part of the relationship — especially physical and/or sexual abuse — difficulty in resolving the grief can be expected.
3. **Mode of death** Grief reactions will be related to how the person died. The method of categorisation was referred to earlier: Natural, Accidental, Suicidal and Homicidal. As might be expected, it is more difficult to resolve grief associated with accidental and unexpected death than with a natural death. Similarly suicide and murder create quite different and often disturbing grief reactions. Because this is such an important issue we will spend more time on this in other lessons. For the present we need to recognise that grief reactions will differ according to the mode of death.
4. **Historical antecedents** What previous experience with loss has the grieving person had and how have they coped? Do they have a history of mental illness — particularly depression? This can be related to the Holmes-Rahe Survey of Recent Experiences. The greater the number of changes, the more difficult the resolution of the loss.
5. **Personality variables** The age and sex of the person and their personality type — How do they cope with stressful events? Are they a dependent person? Do they express their feelings freely? People with particular personality disorders will have a more difficult time and perhaps need specialised help.
6. **Social variables** The social group to which the person belongs, with its cultural attitudes to grief, rituals for mourning, ethnic and religious variables; the support networks available to the mourner; possibility of the secondary gain from being a mourner, making it hard to 'let go' of the role.
7. **Concurrent stresses** Where a high level of disruption occurs following a death, e.g., economic reversals, moving house, school etc.

Next lesson we shall be considering Accidental Deaths.

▶ Conclusion

Ask the students to seek their families' reactions to bereavement using the headings from the Bereavement Study.

UNIT 6: THE IMPACT OF DEATH

LESSON 31
YEARS 11-12

Accidental death

▶ Objective

At the end of this lesson the students will be able:

- to describe the impact of accidental and unexpected death on individuals, families and communities.

▶ Content

Refer to the range of material presented at the last lesson and how many of these were unexpected or accidental deaths.

The following statistics may help students get some idea of the frequency of accidental deaths in Australian society.

Causes of Death — Australia				
1988		\multicolumn{3}{c}{**Age groups**}	
		1–14	**15–24**	**25–44**
Accidents including suicide		45%	53%	23%

		Deaths 1–14 years		
		1986	1987	1988
Accidents / Poisoning / Violence	Male	323	319	302
	Female	187	149	171
Motor Vehicle Accidents (MVAs)	Male	151	130	131
	Female	94	81	76
		Deaths 15–24 years		
Accidents etc.	Male	1378	1383	1493
	Female	391	401	391
MVAs	Male	791	751	765
	Female	249	238	245
Suicide	Male	290	337	388
	Female	71	80	60

Australian Bureau of Statistics

UNIT 6: THE IMPACT OF DEATH

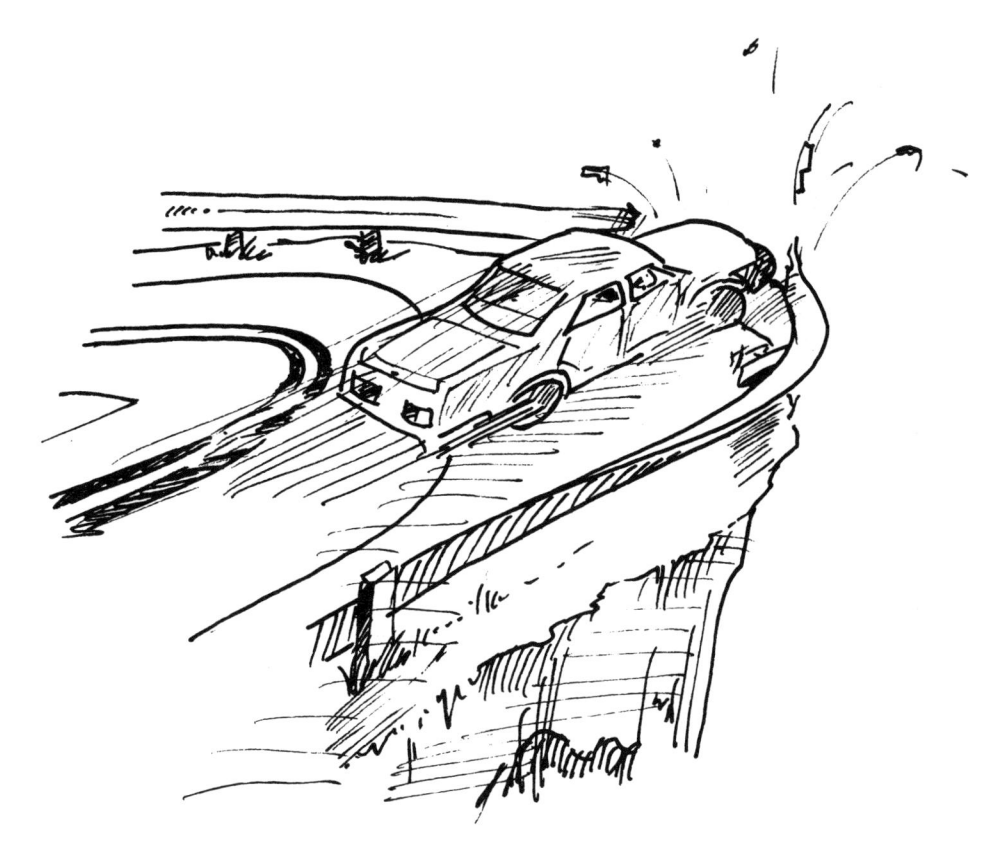

One of the major problems associated with accidental deaths is that there is no time for goodbyes. Any 'unfinished business' that a person has with an individual who dies unexpectedly creates difficulties in the resolution of their grief.

The scenarios on Worksheet 18 from Janice Harris Lord's book *No Time for Goodbyes* reveal the impact on people who lose someone important to them through a tragic, unexpected and often violent death. Following the scenarios some questions are listed... you may have other ones that are more appropriate.

Worksheet 19 offers other material for further discussion.

EXTENSION LESSONS

[If students have not previously covered the material in Section 1, you might take Lessons 10, 13 and 14 at this point.]

Worksheet 18

▶ Scenario 1

Michael, age 19 years.

'Michael was so badly battered — many head injuries. I refused to let his younger brothers go into the hospital room. I regret that now. In an effort to spare them, I robbed them of their last chance to see their brother alive. Even though the casket was closed to the public, our family did get to see and touch his body before the funeral. His brother James, fifteen, slipped one of Mike's special momentoes in his brother's pocket before we closed the lid.'

Questions

Is it important for those closest to the dead person to view the body?
Who should make the decision to view or perhaps not to view the body?
What steps should be taken before people actually go in to view the body, especially when the body has been badly injured?

▶ Scenario 2

Joseph, whose wife, aged 35 years, was killed.

'At 7.30 am my wife died with me at her side, but I never saw her conscious. I have nightmares about that moment even still. I feel I let her down. I wish I could have just looked into her eyes once and said, "I love you".

'Our second Christmas without Michelle is approaching. There are no words that can explain the grief that I and our three children — Erika, seven, Kimberley, five, and Jeffrey, two — have gone through this past year. The two girls still have nightmares. Jeffrey never knew his mother. How can I explain a broken heart and broken dreams?'

Questions

What would you want to say to this father?
How could you help him to make Christmas easier for himself and the children?
Would it be important to explain to the children what happened to their mother? Who would be the best person to do so? Are the nightmares the father and children experiencing normal?
Would Jeffrey, because he is so young, realise what was going on?

▶ Scenario 3

Barbara, death of a parent.

'February 11, 1982 was a very long day — the longest. My mother's surprise visit turned into a tragedy. Now two days later, eyes red, I'm sitting on an airplane flying my mother's body home.

'How do you say to your brothers, "Mum is dead — killed in a needless crash?"'

'I had a rough year and, as always, Mum was coming to comfort me. Now this is Mum's last flight home... It was so quick — so unnecessary — I miss her so much I can hardly bear it.'

Questions

What do you think Barbara would say to her brothers?
What feelings do you think Barbara might have because her mother was coming to 'comfort her'?
How do you think the brothers will react to Barbara?

▶ Scenario 4

Debra, whose brother was killed.

'Dale, I'm just so glad for the time we had together. And I'm glad we were close. But I'm so sad and so sorry we won't have any more laughter or good times together. I will always love you and I will never, ever stop missing you. I just pray that no other brother or sister will ever have to feel the way I feel now. There is an empty space inside of me that can't ever be filled again. No one can take your place.'

Questions

What do you think Debra was doing in writing this letter to Dale?
Do you think she is coming to terms with her grief?

▶ Scenario 5

Ilene, three boys hit by a drunk driver.

'Our three boys were hit by a drunk driver. Dennis and Tim were killed instantly. Jeff survived. It's been six months, and our sixteen-year-old daughter, Pam, still cannot talk about the boys. My husband and Jeff rarely do.'

Questions

What do you think is happening in this family?
What do you think Jeff still feels, being alive when his two brothers died?
Why do you think Pam finds it difficult to talk?
How long does it take to get over grief?

▶ *Scenario 6*

One of the problems with violent death is that the law is involved and frequently people feel they are treated badly. The following is such a situation.

Mary, whose children were killed.

'I contacted the Coroner's Court about two months after my children were killed. I was given the impression that my presence and questions were an imposition to the person handling the case. My children were human beings — not just reports lying on someone's desk.

'Was it wrong for me, their mother, to want to see that the man who killed my children was prosecuted?

'I learned when the trial would be held when it appeared in the newspaper. I wasn't allowed to be in the courtroom because my "presence" might bias the jury. Yet the offender was present throughout the entire trial. The jury never even saw pictures of my beautiful children — and they never knew who I was as I sat alone in the hall the three days of the trial.'

You may wish to get in contact with the Coroner's Court in your city to find out what facilities there are for people such as Mary. Are there social workers, grief counsellors? Is there a referral service?

The Victims of Crime Association operates in some states. Check with the Police Department to see if such a group meets. It may be possible to get a speaker to talk to students.

Death Sculpture: "My Monument to my murdered son".

This summary of an article by David Grogan about Suse Lowenstein reveals the different ways she and the other members of her family coped when Alexander was killed. He was travelling back to the USA on Pan Am Flight 103, December 1988, when a bomb ripped the aircraft apart over Lockerbie, Scotland, killing all 270 people on board and several in Lockerbie, where part of the plane fell.

As you read the article, note your feeling reactions. What aspect of the story had the most impact on you? Did your feelings change during the reading? What other responses did you have?

When Alex Lowenstein, 21, was home from University for the summer vacation of 1988, he willingly posed for his mother, a New York sculptor. Three figures of the virile young surfer were sufficiently completed for his mother to continue her work, using photographs, while Alexander spent the autumn studying in London.

He was due home for Christmas, but at the beginning of December he had a surprise visit from his mother. Suse had felt that she just must see her son and she had dropped everything to travel to London for what turned out to be a wonderful week of sightseeing with him.

On December 21, Suse was working on her sculpture, knowing that Alex's plane would have left London and that he would soon be home! Then the phone rang. A friend of Alex's wanted to know his Pan Am flight number.

"103" Suse replied.

"Oh my God, haven't you heard? That plane just exploded over Scotland," cried the friend. Stunned, Suse reprimanded the girl for playing a morbid joke. Then she collapsed, "I knew," she says, "that Alexander was dead."

The next time Suse saw Alexander was in a dream, three days after the crash. "I was working in my studio, and he was leaning against the door frame," she says. "His face was very white, and he was begging me not to let him go. I woke up and was beside myself."

Suse's despair turned to rage following news reports that the American Embassy in Finland had been tipped off by an anonymous phone caller in early December that terrorists were planning to bomb a Pan Am plane in Europe. US diplomatic personnel were informed of the threat so that they could adjust their Christmas travel plans. Pan Am was also notified, but chose not to tell its customers.

It was the cold end of January before Alexander's remains were returned to America. At Kennedy International Airport the Lowensteins and other grieving families gathered at an area used for handling livestock.

"The rear of a truck opened, and they started unloading coffins with a forklift," Suse recalls. "That's all. Neither Pan Am nor the US Government sent a representative. They showed us no dignity or respect."

By contrast, Suse is grateful to the Scottish police and people of Lockerbie for their heartfelt condolences and their efforts to recover the personal effects of the victims.

"It may seem bizarre," she says, "but I've found myself hungering for every little piece of him." The grisly mementos include torn clothing, half a camera and torn ID cards. The two halves of Alexander's suitcase landed more than 64 kilometres apart, and his windcheater was found 96 kilometres from Lockerbie. Every item was returned washed and handwrapped.

In the months following the bombing, Suse discovered that working on her sculptures of Alexander helped her to make him whole again in her mind.

The finished work is a ring of eight sorrowing figures encircling a woman with one arm draped protectively over her womb and the other stretched heavenward in a gesture of despair.

Suse's greatest fear is that she will somehow forget her son. "I need to speak about him," she says. Her husband Peter has grieved quite differently. He finds it painful to talk about Alexander and values the quiet times alone, flying in his single-engine Piper Dakota.

Both Suse and Peter have been active in a committee formed by relatives of Pan Am Flight 103 victims to lobby for improved airport security measures and to monitor the continuing criminal investigation of the bombing. In August 1991, Peter was part of a delegation that met with British transportation officials and the Scottish police.

UNIT 6: THE IMPACT OF DEATH

LESSON 32
YEARS 11–12

Laughing at death

▸ Objective

At the end of the lesson the students will have:
- examined the role of humour in talking about death.

▸ Content

Introduce the topic, by saying, 'While we see death as sad, sometimes there is humour associated with it. But this can make people feel uncomfortable, for example, the telling of a joke at a funeral service.'

Discuss: What role does humour play in our lives? Some researchers say that it releases pleasure hormones into the body that make us feel good. Hence the saying 'I felt better after a good laugh'.

Ask the class, 'What are some jokes you know that involve death? Or can you recall a sad time where someone said something funny or did something to make the people who were sad, laugh?' Get the class to share these.

Researchers believe that humour functions as a 'social lubricant', that is it enables people to feel relaxed in a social situation. They also believe it acts as a defence mechanism, that is it blocks out difficult feelings and that it helps to gain some sense of control over what might seem uncontrollable.

Recall the jokes and humorous situations that the students related earlier in the lesson. The students are to decide which purpose was intended for their jokes and humorous situations.

Show the ABC video, *Mother & Son*: 'The Funeral', which is a humorous look at the 'Australian way of death'. (This video is available from ABC shops in your state.)

UNIT 6: THE IMPACT OF DEATH

▶ Conclusion

Get the class to try to come to some conclusion about the role of humour by discussing the following statement.

> 'It's all right to make jokes about death so long as you respect the dead and respect people's beliefs about death and dying. But some jokes are in poor taste. Others are downright disgusting. People who laugh at bad jokes must be sick!'

Ask the class to decide if any of the jokes they related were in bad taste and if so, what made them this way?

▶ Conclusion

UNIT 7: EXPLORING YOUR OWN DEATH

LESSON 33
YEARS 11-12

Death and dying

▶ Objectives

At the end of this lesson the students will have:
- explored their own feelings about death and dying;
- examined beliefs about dying.

▶ Content

Woody Allen once made the comment 'It's not that I'm afraid to die, I just don't want to be there when it happens.' And on another occasion, 'I don't want to achieve immortality through my work. I want to achieve it through not dying'.

What do these statements indicate about Woody Allen's attitude to dying?

During this lesson we want to explore some of our attitudes to death and dying and what we believe about death and dying.

(This lesson can be easily divided into two sections.)

Section 1.

Give out the questionnaire (Worksheet 20).

Break the class up into small groups to discuss their responses to these statements. Ask the students to find out what degree of consensus there is in the group.

Allow about 8 to 10 minutes for discussion, then ask the students to report back. Follow up any specific questions that may arise.

Section 2.

Different people have quite different beliefs about death and dying. Ask the students to complete the sentences on Worksheet 21, working individually.

When everyone has completed this task ask the class to share some of their responses. These could be written on the board or on an overhead transparency or photocopied for each student to receive a copy.

Collect all the written statements in order to make a collage of the responses.

UNIT 7: EXPLORING YOUR OWN DEATH

This lesson is likely to stir the emotions and it may be possible for students to do some drawings, make cartoons, write poetry, etc., to give expression to these emotions.

The teacher could play music to show how people have expressed their feelings about death or ask the students to bring records/tapes/CDs to this next lesson. If this does occur, it is important to get the students talking about the music and what it says to them.

▶ Conclusion

Use one of the 'relaxation exercises' from one of the books in the resource section.

Questionnaire

		AGREE	DISAGREE
1.	I have never thought of myself dying in a traffic or plane or some similar accident.		
2.	I often read the obituary items in the paper.		
3.	I see death as involving only a temporary separation from my loved ones.		
4.	I think that medical science is likely to make discoveries that will extend my lifetime twenty or thirty years.		
5.	I seldom think about death or dying.		
6.	I think capital punishment is a cruel and unusual punishment.		
7.	It's always a tragedy when someone dies.		
8.	I expect to face my own death calmly and peacefully.		
9.	Exceptional medical means (drugs, support machines, etc.) should always be used to preserve life no matter what the person's mental condition.		
10.	I find it uncomfortable to think or talk about a person who has died.		
11.	I am both fascinated and frightened to think about having a relationship with someone who may be terminally ill.		
12.	If a person has enough faith, God will always rescue him or her from the threat of death.		

From L. Richards & P. Johnson, *Death and the Caring Community*, Portland, Oregon, Multnomah, 1980.

Worksheet 20

Worksheet 21

Beliefs about dying

1. To me death is...

2. The truth about death for me is...

3. The truth about life for me is...

4. When I am dead I will be...

5. When I die I will feel...

From Brenda Lukeman, *Embarkations*, Englewood Cliffs, N.J., Prentice-Hall, 1982.

Osiris — Egyptian God of the dead

UNIT 7: EXPLORING YOUR OWN DEATH

LESSON 34
YEARS 11-12

The process of dying

▶ Objectives

At the end of this lesson the students will be:
- able to explain the physical process of dying;
- aware of the emotional, intellectual and spiritual concerns of the dying person.

▶ Content

Section 1: The physical process of dying
This lesson can be easily divided into three sections.
Refer back to the last session and what is included on the collage. A great diversity of ideas — are they all correct? are some of them myths — particularly about death? Examine the responses in more detail so that misconceptions can be eliminated.
The physical process of dying will depend greatly on the kind of death. It may be most useful to refer to the major 'killer diseases' in Australian society, e.g. cancer, heart diseases, and accidents. If you feel uncomfortable about dealing with the physical processes of death, invite a doctor or nurse with experience in an Accident and Emergency Unit or a Palliative Care Unit to speak to the class.

Useful references
Therese A. Rando, *Grief, Dying and Death*, Champaign, Illinois, Research Press, 1984.
    (See Chapters 8-13.)
S. Wilcox & M. Sutton, *Understanding Death and Dying*, Palo Alto, Mayfield, 1985.
    (See Chapter 2, 'The Experience of Dying'.)

Section 2: The crisis of knowledge and the expectation of death
Almost everyone expects to live to an old age. When for whatever reason a person's life is 'cut short' there are a variety of different reactions in the person diagnosed as terminally ill and the people who are significant to him/her.
Mansell Pattison calls this the 'crisis of knowledge of death'. From the time of diagnosis to the point of death, the person is in the phase called 'the living-dying interval'. (See the two diagrams describing these phases; these Figures 1 and 2 can be made into overhead transparencies.) Glaser and Strauss have suggested that patients and their significant others will find themselves confronting one of the four Dying Trajectories; for most people it will be either of the first two.

UNIT 7: EXPLORING YOUR OWN DEATH

The four dying trajectories are:

1. certain death at a known time;
2. certain death at an unknown time;
3. uncertain death but a known time when the question will be resolved;
4. uncertain death and an unknown time when the question will be resolved.

Ask the students to consider these four trajectories and what reactions are likely to be in the dying person and those closest to him/her. Write on the board or prepare an overhead with the following:

List under these headings what you think the reactions of the dying person are likely to be:

> **Thoughts**   **Feelings**   **Behaviours**

The students may like to consider:
What differences would there be if the dying person were a child, teenager, young adult, recently married, married person with young children, 35-year-old man in a steady committed relationship with another male, older person?

It is probably best to make a selection from the above list and divide the class into small groups to answer the questions.

For your benefit, information from *Death and the Caring Community* is provided in this lesson to show the focus of concern for those facing 'early death' and the kinds of 'fears' dying people have. It is always helpful to remember the fears the dying person is experiencing will be frequently mirrored in those who are closest to him/her.

Section 3: The dying person's response to death.

At this point it would be useful to introduce a video so that the students can hear from those who are facing death what they think and feel. It will be important that you view the video first so that appropriate questions can be raised for discussion. Some suggested discussion starters are provided with the videos.

A Changed Kind of Reality (35 mins) can be purchased from the University of Sydney Television Service (see list of resources).

Summary: The benefit of this video is that it covers a wide range of age groups from a teenager and young married man, to men and women in their 30s, 40s and 50s. The children and spouses of the dying persons reflect on their thoughts and feelings. The film gives a brief overview of the philosophy and practice of hospice care as expressed at Calvary Hospital, Kogarah.

UNIT 7: EXPLORING YOUR OWN DEATH

▸ Conclusion

Discuss the video. Develop a series of questions that small groups of students can discuss and then report back to the class.

Further discussion material drawn from L. Richards and P. Johnson, *Death and the Caring Community*:

Focus of concern for those facing 'early death'

20s
- leaving the family they love
- how loved ones will cope with grief
- financial and emotional burden on loved ones
- lack of signficant accomplishment

30s
- fear of pain

Women
- her abandonment of the children
- guilt feelings
- not living to see the children grow up

Men
- financial security of the family
- end of productivity
- loss of control

40s
- welfare of the children, spouse
- financial security for survivors
- dread of separation

50s
- welfare of the families
- anxiety concerning drawn out death, personal suffering
- fear of being kept alive beyond hope of recovery

Fears associated with dying

For many people, if not most, fears associated with dying are greater and more pressing than the fear of death. It is important to grasp this fact as we build relationships with those with terminal illness.

Such fears are mentioned in many different studies about death and dying. A search of the literature reveals fears reported time and again. Here's a listing of the most common, drawn from many sources:

- fear of helplessness
- fear of being alone, deserted
- fear of being dead, no one notices
- fear of pain and suffering
- fear of being a burden (two-thirds of those in one study had this fear)
- fear of humiliation (of being seen without wig, unable to control bladder etc.)
- fear of what will happen to projects
- fear of separation from loved ones

UNIT 7: EXPLORING YOUR OWN DEATH

- fear of future for loved ones left behind
- fear of punishment
- fear of impairment, of being unable to care for self
- fear of the unknown
- fear others will have to 'take care of me'
- fears associated with finances
- fears of loss of emotional control, of being 'unable to take it'

Figure 1

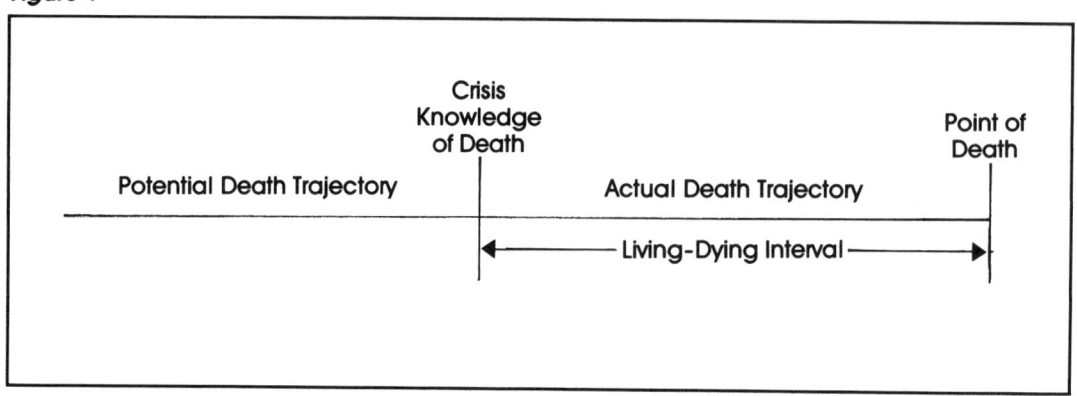

Potential Death Trajectory | Crisis Knowledge of Death | Actual Death Trajectory | Point of Death

Living-Dying Interval

Figure 2

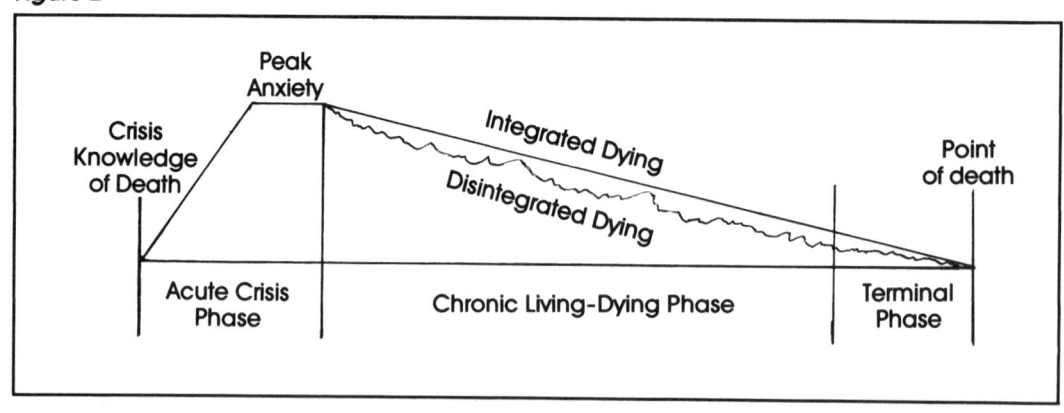

Crisis Knowledge of Death → Peak Anxiety

Integrated Dying / Disintegrated Dying

Acute Crisis Phase | Chronic Living-Dying Phase | Terminal Phase | Point of death

UNIT 7: EXPLORING YOUR OWN DEATH

LESSON 35
YEARS 11–12

People living with and dying from AIDS (1)

▶ Objective

At the end of this lesson the students will:
- have examined the extent of the AIDS epidemic, nationally and internationally, and how this impacts on society.

▶ Content

Prior to the lesson you could prepare a map of the world showing where the problem with AIDS is most evident. (See resource list for information on AIDS.)

A useful book for this lesson is E. Kubler-Ross, *AIDS — The Ultimate Challenge*, New York, Macmillan, 1987.

Say, 'Whilst initially AIDS was thought to be a disease affecting male homosexuals, it is now clear that by far the largest proportion of people suffering from AIDS are heterosexuals'. Using the map, point out those parts of the world where the disease is rampant, for instance parts of central and western Africa, Zaire, Ruanda and Uganda or, on the other side of the world, Haiti. Question the class, 'What is the situation within our own country?' Here it is important to obtain up-to-date facts and figures from your own area.

The local AIDS bureau or AIDS council should be able to provide information. It may be possible for you to get an educator from the AIDS council who can visit the school and conduct a lesson. If this is the case, you will need to indicate what you wish the person to cover in his/her presentation. The most appropriate section for the person to deal with is the factual information contained in the aims for the lesson. The person should also be able to give the information on local resources for people living with AIDS and the support available for people dying from AIDS.

Students could develop graphs showing the way AIDS has affected people at different ages in their life cycle:

  0–5 yrs / 6–10 yrs / 11–15 yrs / 16–20 yrs / 21–25 yrs / 26–30 yrs / 31–35 yrs / 36–40 yrs / over 40 years.

Unit 7: Exploring Your Own Death

Depending on the data available, it may be possible to see the differences between the sexes. Compare the international figures with the national and local... What similarities and differences are evident?

Preparation task for next lesson:

Divide the class into two and for the next lesson ask one group of students to collect information about people living with AIDS. The second group will collect information about people who have died from AIDS. For both groups there are a number of examples, e.g., notables such as Rock Hudson the film star; 'Magic' Johnson the basketball player; Stuart Challender the conductor; Liberace, etc.; cases of haemophiliacs and children; people about whom films have been made or books written.

Ask the students to be prepared to present the information to the class in the form of an interview conducted with the person. If any student actually interviews an HIV positive person, he/she needs to have the person's permission before the information is shared. You may wish to prepare a list of suitable questions which will help the students' research. See next lesson for the kinds of points which could be relevant.

Refer back to last lesson and the Crisis of Knowledge of Death Diagrams (Figures 1 & 2), particularly applicable to patients diagnosed as HIV positive.

▸ Conclusion

Ask, 'As a result of this lesson, what fact have I discovered about AIDS which I did not know before?'

UNIT 7: EXPLORING YOUR OWN DEATH

LESSON 36
YEARS 11-12

People living with and dying from AIDS (2)

▶ Objectives

At the end of this lesson the students will:

- be able to identify the concerns of people living with AIDS;
- be able to express the concerns of people dying from AIDS.

▶ Content

a) People living with AIDS.

Ask the students who found information about people living with AIDS to describe each person, how the information was acquired, the person's thoughts and feelings, or any other information which the person with AIDS expressed. The teacher could write up on the board such things as:

— the gender of the person
— the age of the person
— how long the person has had the disease
— who was most affected by the diagnosis
— the prognosis
— how the person copes.

You will need to have done some personal research if there is only limited information from the students.

Try to get an accurate picture of what it is like for the person living with AIDS. Many talk of the stigma attached to the disease, which effectively isolates them from mainstream society, and the ignorance which is still present in spite of the education programs conducted.

UNIT 7: EXPLORING YOUR OWN DEATH

b) People dying from AIDS.

Question the students who found information about people dying from AIDS. In addition to the above questions you might ask:

— what were the feelings of family, friends, etc., when the person actually died?
— what was the funeral like?
— who attended the funeral?
— how easy was it to grieve openly for the person?
— were people generally supportive?

If there is sufficient time at this point to show the following video (or one similar) and still allow time for discussion, then proceed; otherwise, leave the video for the next lesson.

Video: *A Death in the Family* (approx. 52 mins.) This can be purchased from Ronin Films, Canberra. (See list of resources.)

Summary: Andrew Boyd is the fourth person in New Zealand to have been diagnosed with AIDS. His friends gather round to nurse him through his final days, while his conservative farming family struggles with the tragedy on their own very different terms. The film follows the last 16 days of Andrew's life. On day 16 after the funeral, Simon, one of the friends who has been with him throughout, says he feels the experience has been like visiting a strange and foreign land — part of paradise really, for all its sadness.

Two books which may be of help for this lesson:

Carol Lynn Pearson, *Goodbye, I Love You*, Sydney, Pan Books, 1988.
Betty Clare Moffatt, *When Someone You Love Has AIDS*, New York, Plume Books, 1986.

EXTENSION LESSON

[If students have not previously covered the material in Section 1, you may wish to take Lesson 19 at this point.]

UNIT 7: EXPLORING YOUR OWN DEATH

LESSON 37
YEARS 11–12

Developing an appreciation for life

▶ Objective

At the end of this lesson the students will have:
- contemplated the life they are living now.

▶ Content

Introduce the topic by informing the class of some of Yalom's findings in research work with cancer patients.

'Yalom (1980) found that cancer patients in group therapy had the capacity to view their crisis as an opportunity to instigate changes in their lives. Once they discovered that they had cancer some of their inner changes included:
- a rearrangement of life's priorities — little attention to trivial matters
- a sense of liberation — the ability to choose to do those things they really wanted to do
- an increased sense of living in the moment — no postponement of living until some future time
- a vivid appreciation of the basic facts of life, e.g., noticing the changes in the seasons and other aspects of nature
- a deeper communication with loved ones than before the crisis
- fewer interpersonal fears, less concern over security and more willingness to take risks'*

You can highlight in discussion how people differ in their values as indicated by the priorities they set for their lives and how some people choose to spend time doing the things they like with people they would like to spend time with, while other people do not make this choice. The consideration of death in this activity can act as a positive force to make more sense out of life.

Extension work. Writing your own epitaph

Ask the class 'Is there something you would like to be remembered for? Write down what it is in a few words.' Read out some epitaphs. The students are to design their own tombstones or memorial plaques and to add their epitaphs.

A contemplation of our death can have a profound impact on the sort of lives we live now.

Ask the students to complete Worksheet 22.

* From G. Corey, *I Never Knew I Had a Choice*, Belmont, CA, Brooks-Cole Pub., 1986.

Worksheet 22

My life now*

1. What things in your life make you feel fully alive? Which of these are you currently not doing, but would like to? ....
   ....

2. What do you do well now? What would other people say were your strengths? ....
   ....

3. If you knew you only had twenty-four hours to live, what might you do — would you want to spend the time with people? Or do things alone? How do you feel as you contemplate this last possibility? ....
   ....

4. In what way does thinking about your own death give meaning to your life now? ....
   ....

5. Is there something you would like to accomplish before you die? Is there some underdeveloped potential in you? ....
   ....

6. If you had one last letter to write before you died, who would it be to? What would you say? ....
   ....

7. What I need right now to be a little less afraid of death is ....
   ....

8. What I want from you right now, to help me be a little less afraid is ....
   ....

9. Complete this sentence: As a result of doing this exercise I intend to ....
   ....
   ....

* From G. Corey, *I Never Knew I Had a Choice*, Belmont, CA, Brooks-Cole Pub., 1986.

UNIT 7: EXPLORING YOUR OWN DEATH

LESSON 38
YEARS 11-12

Death awareness

▶ Objectives

At the end of the lesson the students will have:

- examined and discussed their concerns about their own death;
- begun to demonstrate an awareness of their own mortality through participation in class activities.

▶ Content

Ask the students to complete Worksheet 23.

In groups have the students discuss their responses, giving reasons for their choices.

Ask the students as a group how many chose more than one alternative for question 1. 'What does that show about your feelings about death?' Point out that the first four alternatives deal with death as the end of life, whereas alternatives e) and f) deal with the process of dying. Ask the students to reflect on whether their fear is based on the finality of death or the process of dying.

Hand out Worksheet 24, 'Your Personal Death Inventory'. Ask the students to complete it as best they can. In small groups encourage students to share as much or as little of their inventories as they wish.

Worksheet 23

Death awareness

1. What aspect of your own death is the most disturbing to you? Circle one or more.

    a. I could no longer have any experiences

    b. I am worried about what might happen to me after death

    c. My death would cause grief to friends and relatives

    d. All my plans and hopes for the future would come to an end

    e. I am frightened about what might happen to my body after death

    f. Other ....

2. If you had a choice, what kind of death would you prefer? Circle one.

    a. Quiet, dignified death

    b. Death after a great achievement

    c. Death in the line of duty

    d. Suicide

    e. Tragic, violent death

    f. Sudden but not violent death

    g. Of natural causes when I am old

    h. There is no 'appropriate' death

    What do you think has motivated your choice?

    ....
    ....
    ....
    ....
    ....

Your personal death inventory*

1. Would your personal lifestyle change if you were diagnosed as having only a few months to live? If yes, explain what the changes would be ....

2. Do your family and friends discuss death openly? If no, why do you think these discussions are taboo? ....

3. Have you made plans for your funeral? If yes, what are they and have they been communicated to your family? If no, are there some things you would want for your funeral? ....

4. Is there something you would like to do or complete before you die? If so, what is it and why is it important? ....

5. Have you made a will? Are there some prized possessions that you would like to bequeath to someone? Give details ....

6. Do you want to donate any body organs? If so, which? Have you communicated this desire to your family? ....

7. Are there people you would like out thank, express love to, make peace with or praise prior to your death? If yes, who are they, and what do you want to say? ....

* Adapted from J.M. Eddy & W.F. Alles, *Death Education*, St. Louis, C.V. Mosby Co., (1983.)

Worksheet 24

UNIT 7: EXPLORING YOUR OWN DEATH

LESSON 39
YEARS 11-12

Burials and cremations in Australia

▶ Objectives

At the end of this lesson the students will:
- be able to describe the ways in which burials and cremations take place;
- have examined the place of the funeral in Australian society;
- have examined the place of the funeral in various cultures.

Useful reference book for this lesson: Graeme M. Griffin & Des Tobin, *In the Midst of Life: The Australian Response to Death*, Melbourne Uni. Press, 1982.

▶ Content

(This lesson can easily be divided into two sections.)

Section 1.
Prior to this lesson the students should have had the opportunity of visiting a funeral parlour, a cemetery and a crematorium if that is possible. If these visits prove difficult, contact local Funeral Directors and ask if they could come to the school. Many Funeral Directors, particularly those involved with the Australian Funeral Directors Association, have educators and bereavement counsellors on their staff who will happily assist schools. Many of them have very useful resources (see resource list).

If the students are able to visit graveyards they might like to make a note of the epitaphs on the gravestones. They could look at the range of ages — youngest, oldest. The older cemeteries have a lot of historic interest and can provide information on the early life of a settlement in Australia. This work could be planned in consultation with the history department of the school.

The students could discuss what they believe to be the purpose of the funeral.

Does everybody need a funeral? Should the funeral be public or private? For whose benefit is the funeral, the dead or the living?

Guided imagery relaxation activity. (See *You and Stress* in the resource list for choice of relaxation exercises.)

UNIT 8: GRIEF SUPPORT

Section 2.
When the students have completed this and while they still have their eyes closed, say, 'We are going to do an exercise that relates to the topic we have been studying, death and funerals.

'Try to look ahead to the time when you will actually die. Envision the ideal scene of your dying in some detail. Consider the following questions about how you would like your dying to be:

1. How old would you be?
2. Where would you be?
3. What time of day would it be?
4. What special objects would you see as you looked around you?
5. What music would be playing in the background?
6. What would you have been doing with your life just prior to this time?
7. Who would be with you?
8. What would you want to tell them?'

▶ Conclusion

If not already covered in Extension Work, Lesson 37, ask the students to write their own epitaph. They may wish to write it on a headstone they design.

UNIT 8: GRIEF SUPPORT

Extension Lessons
[If students have not previously covered the material in Section 1, you may study Lessons 23, 24 and 25 at this point.]

UNIT 8: GRIEF SUPPORT

▶ LESSON 40
YEARS 11-12

Helping grieving friends and relatives

▶ *Objectives*

At the end of the lesson the students will have:
- identified strategies they can employ to be supportive to grieving people;
- identified possible differences in grieving patterns between males and females.

▶ *Content*

Review with the class people's grief responses.

Ask the class to think of a loss experience that affected them greatly and to recall the following list of coping behaviours. Ask them to indicate by a show of hands which of these they employed.

> Talking to others, talking it through by myself, crying, through support of friends, accepted it as time passed, kept busy, developed new relationships, family support, religious beliefs, by writing or drawing about my feelings, by philosophical beliefs.

If it is a mixed gender class, discuss whether gender differences have appeared in the collation of the class's responses.

Research has identified different grieving patterns in males and females. In general males tend to look at losses involving interpersonal relationships in a problem-solving way; that is, males tend to try to find answers to their grief, whereas females react by exploring their feelings and therefore look for someone to listen to them.

Society tends to focus more on females who are grieving because of the form their grief takes (LaGrande, 1986). Males can be overlooked. They may need to be helped to work through their grief in behavioural rather than verbal ways, yet still be encouraged to deal with feelings. The feelings include the reality of the loss; the failure to explore feeling can prolong grief. Conversely, females may need help with problem-solving. Thus the grief processes of males and females are different, not the feelings.

Unit 8: Grief Support

Divide the class into triads, each group having at least one male and one female (if this is a mixed class). Get the class to discuss the above findings in relation to their own experiences with grieving people.

LaGrande, in a study of the grief experienced by many adolescents, highlighted the following unhelpful strategies when interacting with a grieving person (LaGrande, 1986):

1. Avoidance behaviours — refusing to bring up the subject, or avoiding the person.
2. Directives — 'you will have to be the head of the family now', 'you have to get control of yourself'.
3. Forcing behaviour — being pressured to talk about it, being pressured into new relationships.
4. Judging — 'why are you acting this way?', 'don't take it so hard!'
5. Suggesting full understanding — 'I know exactly how you feel!'
6. Comparing losses — 'at least it is not as bad as...'
7. Random judgments — 'it's for the best', 'she's better off now.'
8. God's needs — 'it was God's will', 'God needed him in heaven'.

(The last strategy may be controversial and could be quite helpful for those people whose faith has not been shaken by the loss.)

Many factors can vary these guidelines, things such as: the context of the statement; what a grieving person expects from the support network; the types of support available, e.g., informational, emotional, practical and social (see Lesson 23); and when the particular type of support is offered, that is, people have different needs at different times in their grieving.

The class can share any experiences similar to those above.

One of the most important things you can do to help grieving people is to listen to them. Hand out copies of Worksheet 25. Ask the class to read it by themselves.

▶ Conclusion

Say that human beings are enormously resilient and with support can overcome great crises. Play the song 'I Will Survive' by Gloria Gaynor. Ask the class to identify the grief response of the singer, that is, how she responds to her broken love affair. What was it that makes the singer a 'survivor'?

Useful reference:
L. LaGrande, *Coping with Separation and Loss as a Young Adult*, Springfield, Illinois, Charles C. Thomas Pub., 1986.

Extension Lesson

[Lesson 27 may be taken before proceeding to Unit 9, if it was not studied in a previous year.]

Listening

When I ask you to listen to me and you start giving advice, you have not done what I asked.

When I ask you to listen to me and you begin to tell me why I shouldn't feel that, you are trampling on *my* feelings.

When I ask you to listen to me and you *do* something to solve my problem, you have failed me, strange as that may seem.

Listen! All I asked was that you listen, not talk or do — just hear me.

Advice is cheap: Twenty cents will get you both Dear Abby and Billy Graham in the same newspaper.

And I can do for myself: I'm not helpless. Maybe discouraged and faltering, but not helpless.

When you do something for me *that I can and need to do for myself,* you contribute to fear and weakness.

But when you accept as a simple fact that I do feel what I feel, no matter how irrational, then I can quit trying to convince you and can get about the business of understanding what's behind this irrational feeling. And when that's clear, the answers are obvious and I don't need advice.

Irrational feelings make sense when we understand what's behind them.

So please listen and just hear me. And, if you want to talk, wait a minute for your turn; and I'll listen to you.

(Author Unknown)

Reprinted with permission, from D. O'Toole, *Growing Through Grief*, North Carolina, Rainbow Connections, 1989.

UNIT 9: THE BIG QUESTIONS

LESSON 41
YEARS 11-12

Self-destructive behaviour: suicide

▶ Objectives

At the end of the lesson the students will:
- be able to identify clues in an individual's behaviour that suggest a need for help to avoid a possible suicide attempt;
- be able to identify the possible thoughts and feelings of someone contemplating suicide;
- be able to devise strategies for helping a friend who is contemplating suicide;
- have identified individuals and agencies that deal with suicide.

▶ Content

Inform the class that the topic for today's lesson is controversial. Some people will think it should not be discussed, because it could encourage the behaviour. For example, opponents of sex education in schools say that by talking freely about sexuality we are encouraging sexual activity. Ask the class, 'What do you think?'

The topic for discussion is suicide. 'Do you think we might be encouraging you to commit suicide if we talk about it? If not, what could we achieve by talking about it?' Ask the class if they think children can commit suicide. (Remind the class that children have a mature concept of death at around age eight.) What reasons would a child have for wanting to take his/her own life? If you were an older brother or sister, what could you do to help? Hand out Worksheet 26 and ask the students to complete it.

In groups the students are to discuss their responses. To draw discussion together, ask which questions caused the most controversy.

Present the students with data on why adolescents commit suicide, e.g. feel unappreciated, series of losses, broken love affair, fear of failure. Ask the class what they think are the reasons. If the students have seen the film *Dead Poet's Society* ask them to state why they think the suicide occurred in the film.

Do we know when someone is going to commit suicide?

UNIT 9: THE BIG QUESTIONS

> **What are the warning signs?**
> giving away prized possessions
> change of lifestyle
> reporting feeling continually depressed
> deteriorating schoolwork
> expressing feelings of helplessness and hopelessness
> talking about suicide
> changes in sleep patterns
> withdrawal from family and friends
> staying away from school, work or other usual activities
> complaints of physical problems when nothing is organically wrong
> loss of self-esteem

▶ Conclusion

Recall the elements involved in helping a grieving person. Say, 'You, too, can be available as a listener to your friends'.

> **What can you do to help?**
> take their discussion about suicide seriously
> don't avoid talking about it
> talk to an adult about it
> let friends know where they can get support
> show the person they have options besides death, even though none of
>   them may seem ideal

Current evidence from the studies with adolescents indicates a relationship between suicide and depression. Teachers should therefore be aware of students who are abnormally quiet and withdrawn as this behaviour may be associated with depression. It is often difficult for young people to ask for help — especially when they are feeling down. At the conclusion of the lesson tell the class that if anyone is feeling upset, disturbed or anxious as a result of what was talked about, or if they have noticed that any of their friends seem disturbed, they should talk to you before leaving the room.

▶ Other projects

1. Collect examples of writing and music that deal with suicide.
2. Explain crisis intervention and how it can be used in suicide prevention programs.
3. Discuss ethical issues — do people have the right to take their own life?

Exploring myths about suicide*

Circle the response which is closest to your view
1. Have you ever seriously thought about committing suicide?
    a. very often
    b. only once in a while
    c. very rarely
    d. never
2. Have you actually attempted suicide?
    a. yes
    b. no
3. Have you known anyone who has committed suicide?
    a. member of immediate family
    b. other family member
    c. close friend
    d. acquaintance
    e. no one
    f. other (specify) ....
4. To what extent do you think suicide should be prevented?
    a. in every case
    b. in all but a few cases
    c. in some cases yes, in other cases, no
    d. in no case: if people want to commit suicide, society has no right to try and stop them

Answer the following true or false questions by circling True or False or Don't Know.

1.	Suicide follows cancer and heart disease as a cause of death for today's youth.	True	False	Don't Know
2.	Suicide is the second leading cause of death amongst youth and young adults.	True	False	Don't Know
3.	Suicide is a problem of communication.	True	False	Don't Know
4.	The best way to help a person who says they don't want to live is to assure them that things will get better and to be patient.	True	False	Don't Know
5.	If a person tells you that he or she wants to kill him/herself and tells you not to tell anyone you should keep this information to yourself so you can show the person you can be trusted and that they have a friend in you.	True	False	Don't Know
6.	The tendency towards suicide is inherited.	True	False	Don't Know
7.	Those who talk about suicide are letting off steam and rarely do it.	True	False	Don't Know
8.	If you thought there was an immediate suicide danger you should leave the person and go for help right away.	True	False	Don't Know

Worksheet 26

9.	If a friend tells you they're thinking of 'ending it soon' give them until tomorrow before you report it to someone or talk more with your friend, since few people who talk about suicide actually attempt it.	True	False	Don't Know
10.	One of the best responses to someone saying, 'I can't take it any more, I think I'm going to kill myself', is to stay calm and ask the person to tell you why they feel that way.	True	False	Don't Know
11.	Once someone decides they want to kill themselves there's really no way to stop them.	True	False	Don't Know
12.	Suicide attempts of any kind should always be considered a cry for help.	True	False	Don't Know
13.	Helplessness and hopelessness are two of the strongest indicators that a person may be or become suicidal.	True	False	Don't Know
14.	Many people attempt suicide through self-destructive behaviours rather than through emotional or verbal signals.	True	False	Don't Know

Quiz answer sheet

1. **FALSE.** Each year more than 2000 young people between the ages of 15 and 24 die as a result of suicide. Only accidents claim more lives. And the ratio may be even higher because many suicides are hidden by families and reported as accidents.
2. **TRUE.** See answer to # 1 above.
3. **TRUE.** People who try to end their own life often do so as a way to gain attention, manipulate other people, or to let others know how desperate and hopeless life is. A person who must resort to suicide to get across these messages has lost the ability to communicate in normal ways. This means the person needs attention. Without it his/her cry will become more desperate and dangerous.
4. **FALSE.** Giving false assurances will not help, and may make the person feel more guilty and worthless. You cannot assure that 'things will get better' although you can let the person know that often things do, and that you believe in their ability to get through their difficult time. It is much better to listen to what the person has to say and to find out why they feel so bad.
5. **FALSE.** You may have to betray a confidence to save a life. Even if you promised not to tell, it is important that you do. This is too big a responsibility to carry alone. Besides most people who tell others are really asking for help. Even if you know it will infuriate the person, you must tell a responsible person as quickly as possible. If the person you tell doesn't take you seriously, and you feel it is serious, tell someone else. Even if you're embarrassed because nothing happened, you did not do wrong by telling. A person who says he/she wants to kill him/herself needs help.
6. **FALSE.** There is no evidence of a genetic link to suicide. However, young people are especially suggestible. A previous suicide of a family member

could establish a destructive model to emulate. Outbreaks of suicide 'clusters' have been noted and it is known that susceptible people already contemplating self-destruction may imitate the suicide actions of their friends or others.

7. **FALSE.** Most of the young people who have attempted or have committed suicide have given verbal clues of their intentions. According to research, adolescents almost always tell of their plans to kill themselves. Sometimes they do so in direct ways, 'I can't take it any more, I'm going to kill myself', and sometimes they give indirect or hidden messages such as, 'They'll be sorry when I've gone,' or 'I won't be a problem to you much longer'.

8. **FALSE.** Do not leave a person alone who you think is in immediate danger of killing him/herself. Stay with the person or find someone else to stay until the crisis passes or until help arrives. If you can't get help in any other way, you may have to call the hospital emergency room, crisis hotline or even the police.

9. **FALSE.** Actually, as stated in # 7, people committing suicide do talk about it before they do it. Also, for every person who commits suicide 50 to 100 more attempt it.

10. **TRUE.** Stay calm and communicate this calmness as best you can. Don't argue or try to prove that the person is acting irrationally or isn't thinking straight. This will only aggravate the situation. LISTEN and sympathise with the person. Encourage the person to talk with you.

11. **FALSE.** Many suicides have been prevented. Most adolescents who think about suicide or have tried it admit later that they didn't want to die — they just didn't want to hurt. Assume the person wants to live even if for the moment the desire is a 'still, small voice.'

12. **TRUE.** See answers above.

13. **TRUE.** Helplessness and hopelessness leave a person with no energy for the present or hope for the future. These two symptoms often mean the person is at high risk and needs attention and support.

14. **TRUE.** Every year many teenagers and young adults die in traffic accidents. It is known that many deaths recorded as accidents are disguised suicides. In studies it has been found that about 25% of the accident victims studied were depressed people with feelings of helplessness and a sense of loss typical of suicidal men and women. Other forms of destructive behaviour that might be called 'passive' suicide attempts are: driving while intoxicated, overeating, excessive dieting, sexual promiscuity, and smoking.

* Adapted and reprinted with permission from D. O'Toole, *Growing Through Grief*, North Carolina, Rainbow Connections, 1989.

UNIT 9: THE BIG QUESTIONS

▶ LESSON 42
YEARS 11-12

Euthanasia

▶ *Objectives*

At the end of this lesson the students will:

- be able to explain the difference between active and passive euthanasia;
- be able to describe the concept of 'dying with dignity';
- have examined the legal aspects of terminating life-sustaining treatment.

▶ *Content*

The most comprehensive report on issues relating to long-term dying patients, including euthanasia, within the Australian context was that undertaken by the Social Development Committee of Victoria. This was produced in April 1987; prior to that, the South Australian parliament introduced the 'Natural Death Act' in 1983.

This South Australian Act gave 'legal recognition to an individual's advance declaration directing the withholding of life-sustaining measures in the event of terminal illness or injury. In summary this Act states that a person of sound mind, 18 years or over, who desires not to be subjected to extraordinary measures in the event of a terminal, irrecoverable illness or injury may make a direction to that end. The direction is to be made before the illness happens, in the prescribed form, witnessed by two people and states that no medical or surgical measures to prolong life be initiated'. (1987:48)

The Victorian committee found a number of shortcomings with the South Australian Act. The students could be asked to discuss what they think are possible shortcomings.

The following is a list of major principles which need to be explored when considering issues about euthanasia:

1. the right to refuse treatment;
2. withdrawal of treatment for both competent and incompetent patients;
3. an individual's request to be allowed to die;
4. informed consent;
5. 'living will' legislation (see *Death Education*, in Resource list for example of 'living will').

UNIT 9: THE BIG QUESTIONS

These principles should be considered alongside the ideas expressed in **'The Dying Person's Bill of Rights'** (Worksheet 27).

The students could be divided into small groups and asked to research one of the five major principles listed above.

▶ Some definitions

EUTHANASIA: Death without suffering — literally a 'good death'.
The word 'euthanasia' can be qualified in four ways:

1. Voluntary Euthanasia: In this case the patient makes a conscious decision that his/her life should end and asks for help in doing so. This is sometimes called 'assisted suicide';
2. Involuntary Euthanasia: In this instance, society, or an individual in society, makes a positive decision to end the life of someone suffering without asking consent from the sufferer;
3. Active Euthanasia: This implies that some active step, for example the giving of a drug, has been taken to cause the death of the sufferer;
4. Passive Euthanasia: In this case no *active* treatment is given, rather treatment is withheld, for example, an infection occurs and no treatment is given.

Though euthanasia is discussed in relation to many illnesses and age groups, it is most commonly associated with severe mental and/or physical disability or in relation to severe suffering, usually pain. Malformed children or abnormal children or people with terminal illness are usually the subjects of discussion.

ACTS AND OMISSIONS:

1. To accelerate the process of death = 'killing'
2. To withhold treatment which could prolong life = 'letting die'.

Could be thought morally indefensible to 'kill' patients but morally acceptable to withhold treatment.

In the Netherlands voluntary euthanasia is practised, though to what extent is not known. The legal position in Holland still seems ambiguous. The country's medical position is that:

1. every patient has the right to ask for euthanasia;
2. every doctor has the right to perform euthanasia;
3. every doctor has the right to refuse;
4. the patient is the only one who can decide — the doctor and the family cannot make the decision for that patient.

EXTENSION LESSON

Class debate. Possible topics:

The doctor's duty is to sustain life but this should not result in the prolongation of suffering.

The right to live should be balanced by the right to die.

Worksheet 27

The Dying Person's Bill of Rights*

I have the right to be treated as a living human being until I die.
I have the right to maintain a sense of hopefulness, however changing its focus may be.
I have the right to be cared for by those who can maintain a sense of hopefulness, however changing this might be.
I have the right to express my feelings and emotions about my approaching death in my own way.
I have the right to expect continuing medical and nursing attention even though 'cure' goals must be changed to 'comfort' goals.
I have the right not to die alone.
I have the right to be free from pain.
I have the right to have my questions answered honestly.
I have the right not to be deceived.
I have the right to have help from and for my family in accepting my death.
I have the right to die in peace and dignity.
I have the right to retain my individuality and not be judged for my decisions which may be contrary to the beliefs of others.
I have the right to discuss and enlarge my religious and/or spiritual experiences, whatever these may mean to others.
I have the right to expect that the sanctity of the human body will be respected after death.
I have the right to be cared for by caring, sensitive, knowledgeable people who will attempt to understand my needs and will be able to gain some satisfaction in helping me face my death.

* This Bill of Rights was created at a workshop on 'The Terminally Ill Patient and the Helping Person' in Lansing, Michigan, sponsored by the Southwestern Michigan Inservice Education Council and conducted by Amelia J. Barbus, Associate Professor of Nursing, Wayne State University, Detroit.

Question: With every Declaration or Bill of Rights there are accompanying responsibilities — with whom do the responsibilities for implementing these rights rest? ....
....
....
....
....
....
....
....

UNIT 9: THE BIG QUESTIONS

LESSON 43
YEARS 11–12

The quality of life

▸ Objectives

At the end of this lesson the students will have:
- explored some 'quality of life' ethical dilemmas;
- participated in the process of ethical decision making.

Useful reference
B. Kozier & G. Erb, *Fundamentals of Nursing: Concepts and Procedures*, Redwood City, California, Addison-Wesley, 1983.

▸ Content

Last lesson we explored the problems associated with the patient's 'right to die' and were confronted with the ethical dilemmas surrounding this decision.

An excellent resource for this lesson is the film, now on video, *Whose Life Is It, Anyway?* Richard Dreyfus plays the part of a sculptor who is involved in a near fatal accident. He is left paralysed from the neck down. The story is of the battle between the medical authorities whose aim is to prolong and sustain life and his desire to die. It raises many issues and sensitively explores changing relationships, dependence-independence, power struggles, etc.

If time does not permit the class to see the video, it is possible to do the exercise on Worksheet 28 using the 'Life-death dilemma for twins' on the Worksheet, in which ethical issues are raised.

Resolving an ethical dilemma is never easy, particularly when team members may have quite different attitudes and values. To assist the process, then, clear guidelines need to be established.

Students will work through Worksheet 28 on the basis of the video or the article.

Divide the class into groups to do the exercise and at the conclusion ask each group to report back. Discuss the differences between groups, and any other issue that arises.

▸ Conclusion

Ask, 'What is something new I have learned as a result of this lesson?'

Worksheet 28

To resolve an ethical dilemma

1. Establish a sound database:
   — what persons are involved?
   — what is their involvement?
   — what is the proposed action and its intent?
   — what are the consequences of the proposed action?

2. Identify the conflicts presented by the situation.

3. Outline alternative actions to the proposed course of action.

4. Outline the consequences of the alternative actions.

5. Determine the ownership of the problem and the appropriate decision maker:
   — who should make the decision and why?
   — for whom is the decision being made?
   — what criteria (social, economic, psychological, physiological or legal) should be used in deciding who makes the decision?
   — what degree of consent is needed by the subject (patient or other)?
   — what, if any, moral principles (rights, values) are enhanced or negated by the proposed action?

6. Define the health care worker's obligation.
   Examples:
   a. To maximise the patient's well being.
   b. To balance the patient's need for autonomy and family members' responsibilities for their patient's well-being.
   c. To support each family member and enhance the family support system.
   d. To carry out hospital policies.
   e. To protect other patients' well-being.
   f. To protect the health care worker's own standards of care.

'Life-death dilemma for twins'

by Peter Steiner

Doctors face a surgical and ethical minefield in deciding the fate of Sydney's six-day-old siamese twins.

The twin boys, Brendon and Peter, have come through their first trip to the operating theatre and yesterday were placed on oxygen.

Yesterday's operation was to create an external opening for shared bowels.

But the boys' young parents and doctors face many agonising decisions regarding further surgery as tests reveal the full extent of their shared organs.

The awful dilemma confronting doctors is that surgical separation may be fatal for either or both boys.

What the twins share:
- Possibly the liver
- Genitals
- Some pelvic bone
- Legs
- One arm but two hands off it

Apart from the surgical risks, the ethical decisions include:
- Whether one twin should survive at the expense of the other.
- Whether they should be separated at all.
- What quality of life could one of the malformed children expect after such an operation.

The twins, born by Caesarean, are recorded and treated as two patients in the neonatal intensive care unit of Camperdown Children's Hospital.

They share a common lower body from the chest down.

Tests show the twins have two stomachs, two small intestines, a shared bladder and large intestine, a complex fused pelvis, common arteries leading to the legs and an abnormal third arm arising out of the joined section.

Although this arm has two hands it lacks a humerus, the long bone from shoulder to elbow.

The boys' brains control one leg each via two separate spinal cords, meaning that any surgical survivor could never have anything more than one functional leg at best, even if one twin were sacrificed.

Recreating a viable gut, urinary tract and abdominal wall are among the difficulties facing paediatric surgeons caring for the boys.

Friday's surgery corrected an imperforate anus.

The twins developed breathing difficulties following surgery and have been placed on oxygen therapy. One twin has been found to have a heart defect.

Surgeons will delay decisions on treatment pending test results and discussions of options with the parents.

Siamese twins are identical twins formed by the fusion of a single ovum and sperm, but in which the fertilised egg incompletely divides after conception.

From the *Sun Herald*. Used with permission.

Summary of facts to assist in decision making:

Twins share a common lower body from chest down.

Twins have:

> two stomachs,
> two small intestines.

Twins *share:*

> a bladder and large intestine,
> complex fused pelvis,
> common arteries leading to the legs,
> an abnormal third arm (has two hands but lacks a humerus).

Boys' brains control one leg each via two separate spinal cords.
One twin has been found to have a heart defect.

(Details taken from preceding article in the *Sun Herald* by P. Steiner.)

UNIT 9: THE BIG QUESTIONS

LESSON 44
YEARS 11-12

Organ transplantation

▶ Objective

At the end of this lesson the students will have:
- explored the implications of organ transplantation.

▶ Content

Prior to this lesson contact the Red Cross in your capital city to obtain copies of the pamphlet on organ donation entitled, *Go On! Say Yes to the Red Cross Transplant Program.*

Ask the class to name any person they can recall who was the recipient of a transplant. The most likely person to be mentioned, because of her media coverage, will be Fiona Coote. How many of the students have agreed to donate their organs? What about other members of their family? Has it ever been discussed? Have they signed the agreement on their driver's licence?

What organs can be used in a transplant?
Kidneys, corneas, heart, lungs, liver and pancreas.

Of these the organ that creates the most emotive reactions is the heart. Get the class to think of the way in which the heart is used symbolically in the English language to express emotion, e.g. 'I love you with all my heart' etc.

In our society today, most of the focus is on the recipient of the organ and little on the donor family.

In the early stages of the transplant program at St. Vincent's Hospital, Sydney, one of the social workers wrote an article, 'Alpha and omega: the grief of the heart donor family'. She wrote it because she was concerned about the lack of support for donor families.

One of the authors of this book has been involved in counselling families and very frequently their grief is both delayed and distorted. The gift of the organ which gives life to another person usually means the death of the donor. Most donors are young people accidentally and unexpectedly killed, whose families or partner have to make the decision, while still in a state of shock, to allow the organs to be used.

The article on Worksheet 29 appeared in the daily press: 'Organ transplant doctors "insensitive to donor families"'. Ask the students to discuss it.

Unit 9: The Big Questions

Russell Scott, a Sydney lawyer, wrote about the trade in human organs in Third World countries. The article is on Worksheet 30 and it provides a different view of the transplant debate. Get students to discuss the issue from the point of view of the impoverished Third World person trying to keep his family alive. Selling organs is one means by which the family can raise some money.

Ask the students to close their eyes as you read the following:

'It is the early hours of Saturday morning and you are fast asleep. You are awakened by a knocking sound, can't quite work out whether you are still dreaming or not. Gradually it dawns on you that it is the front door, and you get out of bed to answer it, wondering who it could possibly be at that hour of the night.

'You go towards the door and see your parents with a policeman and policewoman who are coming into the house. They suggest you all sit down as they have some bad news. Your older brother and his girlfriend were both involved in a serious accident and your brother has been killed. Your parents are asked to go to the hospital to identify the body.

'At the hospital the doctor and nurse explain what has happened and that your brother would have died instantly from the injury. The girlfriend is in a serious but stable condition in Intensive Care. They now ask whether your parents are happy for your brother's organs to be used for a transplant. Your brother had signed his licence, the tissues have been matched and there is a person in urgent need of a heart transplant'.

▶ Questions

What would be your response?
What would be the response of your parents?
How do you think you would feel?
What sort of thoughts would go through your mind?
How easy would it be for you to make the decision? What if your decision was different from your parents?

▶ Conclusion

Mexico announced recently that it was considering giving a special award to people who are organ donors. Do you think this has merit and would be something the Australian government could consider?

▶ Reference

S. Pitman, 'Alpha and Omega: The grief of the heart donor family,' *Med J Aust*, Vol. 143, December, 1985, pp. 568–570.

ARTICLE: 'Organ transplant doctors "insensitive to donor families"'*

by Suzanne McDonnell

Three years ago, Mrs Josie Beyer consented to donate the organs of her brain-dead son to someone who needed them.

Today she said she was still bitter at the insensitive way doctors approached her and her family for his organs.

According to a prominent medical ethicist, the Beyer case is similar to that of many families who have donated a dead relative's organs for transplant operations.

Mrs Beyer's 18-year-old son, Simon, was taken to a leading Melbourne hospital with serious head injuries after he was hit by a car on New Year's Eve.

A doctor came to see the Beyer family as they sat in the nearby waiting room, awaiting news of an improvement in Simon's condition.

Simply and efficiently the doctor explained that Simon was brain-dead and asked if the family would consider donating his organs.

'He explained it in a detached manner. He was not at all compassionate. It was an awful shock to be asked something like that. It reels you against the wall,' Mrs Beyer said yesterday.

The family consented and signed a form and they were left to go home.

Mrs Beyer said that although she was pleased that Simon's organs had gone to help someone else, she and her husband had suffered many months of torment over the decision. They received no follow-up contact or support from the hospital.

Mr Nicholas Tonti-Filippini, a former director of the St Vincent's Bioethics Centre in Melbourne and now advisor to the Australian Catholic Bishop's Conference in Canberra, said the organ retrieval process had become a 'technological fix' dominated by the need for speed in performing the transplant.

'The nature of the technology is such that it dominates the whole transplant process,' Mr Tonti-Filippini said.

Because of his ethical concerns about organ harvesting, Mr Tonti-Filippini, who suffers renal failure, refuses to have a kidney transplant.

He said transplant technology was so complex and urgent that the feelings of relatives for donors and recipients were often overlooked.

* from the *Sydney Morning Herald*. Used with permission.

ARTICLE: 'Trade in Transplants'

by Jane Southward

A Sydney lawyer has been selected to join an international probe into the macabre and sometimes murderous trade in human organs for transplant.

If you described Russell Scott as a troubleshooter you would probably be doing the man a disservice. He is more than that.

In the field of bioethics he has taken on challenges that have proved too daunting for many world authorities; challenges such as writing new laws defining life and death.

Fifteen years ago Mr Scott threw in his lucrative job as a senior partner in one of Australia's biggest law firms to join a top-level inquiry into the ethics of human tissue transplantation.

Next he worked solidly on the NSW Law Reform Commission's inquiry into in vitro fertilisation, concerning himself with the definition of the beginning and ending of life.

Now the Mosman father-of-six is set to join the World Health Organisation inquiry into the international trade of body organs and tissues.

Mr Scott admits it is all heavy stuff.

"I was approaching 50 when I realised there ought to be more to being a lawyer than making money," he said.

Brain death redefined

"I had been practising as a commercial partner for 15 years in a top firm when I decided I wanted to put something back into the community."

He still laughs when he recalls he stumbled upon an issue that changed his life, while working with Justice Michael Kirby and Sir Zelman Cowen on the Australian Law Reform Commission's inquiry into human organ transplants.

"We were splitting up the references to see who would do hat and someone said, 'We've got this one on human tissue transplantation' and everyone wanted to avoid it like the plague so I said, 'I'll have a go'," he recalled.

"Then it suddenly hit me what an extraordinary project it was because it was a project in which we redefined death, the concept of brain death."

Mr Scott's latest project — the WHO inquiry into international trade in body parts such as kidneys, hearts and livers — is expected to be as sinister as it is stimulating.

An international conference in Canada in August heard allegations of "fattening houses" in South America in which people are fattened up and then killed for the use of their organs in transplants.

The International Commission of Health Professionals told the conference the trade in body parts was lucrative because the demand was far greater than the supply.

The ICHP, based in Switzerland, said evidence included reports of cemeteries containing bodies of children with missing body parts, financial incentives which favour illegal trafficking, and false birth certificates and travel documents.

Better documented cases have hit the British press, including recent allegations that Turkish migrants have been lured by promises of instant wealth and work if they donate their kidneys to sick millionaires.

One donor, a peasant who had been trying to support his wife and four children working in Istanbul's sewers for $1 a day, told a British inquiry in December that he was promised he could earn enough money in Britain to buy a Mercedes car.

The peasant agreed to go to London for what he thought was a hotel job. When he was admitted to a private hospital he was not suspicious; it was so luxurious he assumed it was a hotel.

The man, who speaks no English, signed a form for what he thought were blood tests required as part of the vetting procedure for his job. In fact he had signed a consent form allowing surgeons to remove a kidney which was transplanted to a wealthy Libyan doctor.

It is cases like this that Russell Scott and the WHO committee will investigate.

"Most Western countries have introduced modern legislation to regulate transplantation," he said.

"In Australia it is illegal for money to change hands.

"But there is growing evidence of a black market operation in other parts of the world. It has been claimed people have been fattened up and then killed for their organs and tissues.

No trade in Australia

"This murderous use for human beings is unacceptable by any standards."

In Australia there had been no evidence of a commercial trade of organs such as kidneys, livers and hearts, Mr Scott said.

That the WHO has sought Australian advice on possible laws to prevent the scandalous trade is clearly due to Mr Scott's experience in medical and research ethics.

In 1977, a year before the world's first IVF baby was born in Britain, Mr Scott was part of a committee that recommended new laws to regulate the use of technology to create human life.

* from the *Sydney Morning Herald*. Used with permission.

Resource list

▶ *Videos*

For general information contact:

Funeral and Bereavement Educators' Association (FABEA)
    722 High Street
    East Kew Victoria 3012
    Telephone: (03) 859 0299

For a listing of those funeral companies throughout Australia involved in FABEA, contact their National office. Most of the funeral companies involved with FABEA offer some support and educational services.

Contact the funeral companies in your area to find out what support and educational services they may offer. You may find you can obtain videos, books etc. locally.

Some excellent videos are listed below, together with where-to-hire information and running time where provided.

A bolt from the blue   JA/M*
This South Australian film is about a group of teenagers/early 20's who have experienced trauma such as the death of parent/s, bushfires, life-threatening illness, motor accident, etc. and they share their ways of coping with the grieving process. This film aids discussion with young and old alike.

A changed kind of reality
Running time: 35 minutes
This moving production explores sympathetically and honestly the differing experiences of people with incurable diseases.

A death in the family   Ronin Films (06) 248 0851
                                                                                      PO Box 1005
                                                                                      Civic Square
                                                                                      ACT 2608

Running time: 52 minutes
Andrew Boyd is the fourth person in New Zealand to have been diagnosed with AIDS. His friends gather round to nurse him through his final days, while his conservative farming family struggles with the tragedy on their own very different terms. The film follows the last 16 days in Andrew's life. On day 16, after

Resource List

the funeral, Simon, one of the friends who has been with him throughout, says he feels the experience has been like visiting a strange and foreign land: 'Part paradise really, for all its sadness'.

Dad's girl   Breakthrough series — Film Australia 1989
Running time: 11 minutes
Janea's parents divorced when she was six years old; she is now fourteen. In the film she describes her feelings of loss and the affinity she feels for her absent father and her Maori heritage. Janea tells how her schoolwork initially suffered after the separation and how she still sometimes gets depressed and misses her father.

Death of a child   JA/M*
An Adelaide Children's hospital production raising a number of issues surrounding sudden death, and death following a terminal illness in childhood. Based around group discussions involving health professionals, a mother whose child died of leukaemia, and parents of an infant who died a cot death.

Eric's story: Walk in the world for me.   JA/M*
A tender story of a young man's struggle against leukaemia. His mother narrates this honest film, sharing much of the strength engendered during these critical years. Ideal for high school students because they see someone their own age struggle with the problem of dying. An excellent film on an individual and his family's way of dealing with the dying process.

Fragile time
Running time: 28 minutes
Young people at risk of suicide send out warning signals. This powerful program will enable viewers to learn to recognise these signals and to intervene before it is too late.

From the other side   Centacare Family Welfare, Sydney, 1987
Running time: 16 minutes
This is a video recording of young people in a Sydney high school. They met and talked with each other and a youth worker about their thoughts and feelings, when their parents separated, as they adjusted to their changing family situation. The participants are not actors. The 'live' recording means that occasionally some of the young people's comments are difficult to hear. Nevertheless, the video is a realistic portrayal of the emotional pain experienced by adolescents, and is an excellent discussion starter.

In loving memory   Breakthrough series — Film Australia, 1989
Running time: 14 minutes
The video recounts the story of fourteen-year-old Mary, who was diagnosed with cancer whilst still in primary school. Now in remission, she recalls her feelings, her changed relationships with peers and the things that helped her cope.

Let out the darkness   JA/M*
Running time: 28 minutes
The rights, options and responsibilities of the survivors are explored together with the role of the funeral director and the purpose of the funeral service. The theme of the film is that mourning customs are designed to 'let out the darkness'.

Resource List

No-one wants to talk about it
Running time: 29 minutes
Interview with a dying patient. He is angry at what he sees as a lack of consideration for his particular needs.

Surviving broken relationships
Running time: 21 minutes
Clayton Barbeau identifies the signs of depression, that is, changes in eating and sleeping habits, inattentiveness, a sense of alienation and even thoughts of suicide. The personal stories and true-to-life examples illustrate how the suggested tactics of survival can work.

Surviving life transitions
Running time: 26 minutes
Clayton Barbeau talks about the many experiences of change that make up daily living. Some of these changes can be very threatening. Stories and strategies offer a guide for healthy personal growth.

Surviving grief
Running time: 24 minutes
Clayton Barbeau helps the viewer understand the grieving process and work toward acceptance of the loss of a loved one. He emphasises the importance of giving permission to 'feel', be it tears, loneliness, or anger, and suggests we don't prolong and nurture grief but take one day at a time.

The fall of Freddie the leaf
Running time: 16 minutes
This inspiring allegory by Dr. Leo Buscaglia is the tale of a journey through life, which highlights the delicate balance between death and life. It helps children and adults celebrate the changes of nature and accept the season of death.

Three segments of grief   JA/M*
Produced by Rusden College, Melbourne, after the death of three students:

1) **Death means forever**
   A widow expresses her feelings after the death of her husband in a boating accident.
2) **Life after Nepal**
   The family of a student killed in a climbing accident talk about their responses to death.
3) **The final statement**
   Students express their feelings in response to the suicide of one of their classmates.

Visions of hope — The 'Near Death' experience
Running time: 40 minutes
A documentary on the near death experience, this video makes no claims, but endeavours to examine the issue. Suitable for using in short excerpts, it offers a means of raising discussion on the whole issue of the fear of death and dying.

RESOURCE LIST

6.09 to Granville   JA/M*
Excellent documentary on the Granville train disaster.

* John Allison/Monkhouse Support Services (JA/M)
   379 Burke Road
   Camberwell Victoria 3146
   Telephone: (03) 889 0299

▶ *Books for Adolescents*

Blume, J. (1983) *Tiger Eyes*. London, Pan Piccolo Books. (An adolescent girl witnesses her father's death. The book shows how different people react.)

Lloyd, C. (1989) *The Charlie Barber Treatment*. London, Julia MacRae. (An adolescent boy struggles to cope with his mother's death.)

Paterson, K. (1977) *Bridge to Terabithia*. New York, Avon Books. (Shows how Jess copes with the death of his friend Leslie.)

Pershall, M.K. (1988) *You Take the High Road. Losing someone you love is only the beginning*. Ringwood, Victoria, Penguin Plus. (Sam experiences a series of losses, moving house, her grandmother going away, the death of her baby brother and the subsequent separation of her parents.)

Shaw, B. (1990) *So Mum & Dad Split Up. Coping when parents separate and divorce*. Ringwood, Victoria, Puffin Books. (A book to help adolescents cope with their parents' divorce.)

Stewart, M. (1985) *Miranda's Story*. Ringwood, Victoria, Puffin Plus. (Describes how an adolescent handles her hospitalisation and treatment for cancer.)

Talbert, M. (1988) *Dead Birds Singing*. Ringwood, Victoria, Penguin Books. (This book describes how Matt survives a car crash in which his mother dies, his sister is injured and subsequently dies, leaving him to be cared for by family friends.)

Viorst, J. (1971) *The Tenth Good Thing About Barney*. New York, Atheneum Press. (This book presents the reaction of a grief-stricken young girl whose cat Barney has died. An excellent discussion starter for high school students.)

Williams, G. & Ross, J. (1983) *When People Die*. Edinburgh, Macdonald Publishers. (A brief, factual book about reactions to death, the funeral and how to cope.)

Zagdanski, D. (1990) *Something I've Never Felt Before. How teenagers cope with grief*. Melbourne, Hill of Content. (A book that mixes the author's advice with direct comments from young people about their experiences.)

Resource List

▸ Books for Teachers and Parents

Appleby, M. & Condonis, M. (1990) *Hearing the Cry. Suicide prevention*. Narellan, New South Wales, R.O.S.E. Education, Training and Consultancy. (Advice for parents, teachers and other professionals about suicide.)

Eddy, J.M. & Alles, W.F. (1983) *Death Education*. St. Louis, C.V. Mosby Co. (Good background text.)

Fabian, S. (1986) *The Last Taboo*. Ringwood, Victoria, Penguin. (Basic text on suicide.)

Gordon, A. & Klass, D. (1979) *They Need to Know. How to teach children about death*. Englewood Cliffs, N.J., Prentice Hall. (Basic text.)

Hodgkinson, P.E. & Stewart, M. (1991) *Coping with Disaster. A handbook of disaster management*. London, Routledge. (Basic text on disaster management aimed at community disaster, but principles could be extrapolated for schools.)

Jewett, C. (1984) *Helping Children Cope with Separation and Loss*, U.K. Batsford Academic and Educational.

LaGrand, L.E. (1986) *Coping with Separation and Loss as a Young Adult*. Springfield, Illinois, Charles C Thomas Pub. (Good background information on reactions of older adolescents.)

Lord, J.H. (1988) *Beyond Sympathy*. Ventura, California, Pathfinder Publishing. (What to say and do for someone who is grieving).

———. (1988) *No Time for Goodbyes. Coping with sorrow, anger and injustice after a tragic death*. Sydney, Millennium Books. (Focuses on the unique grief and shock that follows the sudden violent death of a loved one.)

Macnab, F. (1989) *Life After Loss. Getting over grief, getting on with life*. Sydney, Millennium Books. (Effective strategies for coping with death, broken relationships and other shattering personal losses.)

McKissock, D. and M. (1989) *In My Own Way: The Bereavement Journal*. Sydney, Millennium Books. (A beautiful, illustrated journal with helpful explanations on how to use it effectively.)

McKissock, M. (1985) *Coping with Grief*. Sydney, Australian Broadcasting Commission. (Concise, straightforward account of grief reactions.)

Montgomery, B. & Evans, L. (1984) *You and Stress*. Ringwood, Victoria. Penguin Books. (Some good relaxation exercises.)

Raphael, B. (1985) *Anatomy of Bereavement. A handbook for the caring professions*. London, Hutchinson and Co. (Essential professional reading.)

Raphael, B. (1986) *When Disaster Strikes*. London, Hutchinson and Co. (Basic text on disaster management.)

Simplicity Funerals. (1990) *Things You Need to Know About Funerals*. (Available from your local branch. Basic information about funerals.)

Wass, H. & Corr, G.A. (1982) *Helping Children Cope with Death. Guidelines and Resources*. Washington, D.C., Hemisphere Pub. Co. (Good background for teachers.)

Wells, R. (1988) *Helping Children Cope with Grief. Facing a death in the family*. London, Sheldon Press. (Straightforward advice for nurses, teachers, doctors, parents and friends.)

Resource List

Worden, J.W. (1991) *Grief Counselling and Grief Therapy* 2nd edition, New York, Springer. (Excellent text on bereavement counselling.)

Yang, W. & Pip, C. (1990) *Bodywork. Confessions from the funeral trade.* Sydney, Hale and Iremonger. (Good background; pictorial details of the funeral trade.)

▶ Services

Many funeral companies (particularly members of the Funeral and Bereavement Educators' Association/FABEA, 722 High Street, Kew, Victoria 3012), offer support and some educational services.

The National Association for Loss and Grief (NALAG) has a branch in each state in Australia. Additionally some states have local chapters. This can be your contact for information about other agencies and support groups.